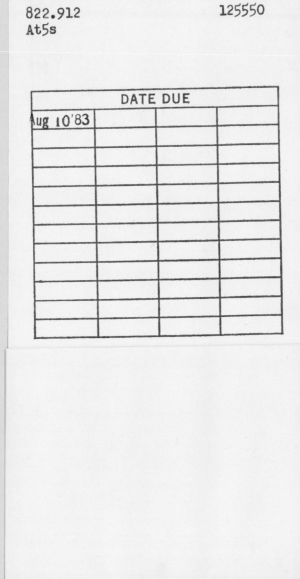

SEAN O'CASEY
From Times Past

Also edited by Robert G. Lowery

SEAN O'CASEY: CENTENARY ESSAYS (with David Krause)
ESSAYS ON SEAN O'CASEY'S AUTOBIOGRAPHIES
O'CASEY ANNUAL No. 1

SEAN O'CASEY
From Times Past

by
Brooks Atkinson

Edited by Robert G. Lowery

BARNES & NOBLE BOOKS
TOTOWA, NEW JERSEY

First published in the U.S.A. 1982 by
BARNES & NOBLE BOOKS
81, Adams Drive, Totowa,
New Jersey, 07512

ISBN 0-389-20005-0

Printed in Hong Kong

822.912
 At5s
12 5-5-5 0
July 1983

To Maureen Murphy
who was my Lady Gregory

Contents

Acknowledgements

The author, editor and publisher wish to thank *The New York Times* for kindly giving permission for the use of the copyright material (© 1926–1964 by The New York Times Co.). They also wish to thank Al Hirschfeld for the use of his drawings of Brooks Atkinson and Sean O'Casey for the jacket (© 1981 Al Hirschfeld).

Introduction

When Brooks Atkinson left his position in 1960 after thirty-five years as drama critic for the *New York Times*, he left behind a legacy of outstanding journalism. He was called 'the most respected, most influential and perhaps the most quoted drama critic in the United States'. His high standards of theatrical reporting influenced numerous writers, including many of his own colleagues on rival newspapers. Scholars and literary historians interested in modern drama have since discovered his past reviews to be an unlimited source of perceptive insights into the history and development of New York theatre and twentieth-century drama.

The son of a newspaperman, the critic was born to be a journalist. While studying at Harvard University he wrote articles on George Bernard Shaw which appeared in the Boston *Herald*. For a brief time afterwards he was a reporter for the *Daily News* in Springfield, Massachusetts. He taught English for a year at Dartmouth College, but in 1918 he returned to journalism as a reporter and assistant to the drama critic of the Boston *Transcript*. In 1922 he joined the *Times* as editor of the book review section.

Atkinson took over 'The Play' column from Stark Young in 1925. For the next thirty-five years, except for the Second World War years, that column was his column, and to theatregoers it was as much a fixture on the *Times* as the old English lettering on the masthead. During the war he was a correspondent for his paper in China and later in Moscow, where his reporting won him a Pulitzer Prize for Journalism in 1947. Returning to drama criticism in September 1946 Atkinson continued his column until 1960. For five years more he wrote a twice-weekly column, 'Critic at Large'.

For Atkinson drama criticism was a form of reporting. The theatre was news, and he reported it just as financial columnists reported the stock market fluctuations. The primary difference between the two functions was that drama criticism made no pre-

1

tence to objective reporting. Whereas objectivity was drummed
into the heads of cub reporters and was an element displayed by
the best journalists, subjectivity ruled the critic's reasoning
because theatre reporting was more a judgement of values than a
compilation of facts. The judgement was based on many factors,
but no matter how it was worded it usually came down to personal opinions.

'There is no such thing as being right or wrong about any form
of art,' Atkinson once wrote. 'There are only personal opinions.
No two people think alike or have the same emotional responses
to a work of art.' In his opinion everything hinged on one question: 'Is it a good play or not? It may have the grandest of themes.
It may have a glamorous cast. Both of these elements can be
reported. But if play and performance do not arouse some emotional or intellectual responses in the theatregoer, they are worthless because they do not fulfil the primary function of the theatre.
They are as lifeless as the scenery that is carted away after a flop.'
To Atkinson the interaction between play and audience was of
paramount importance in deciding the merits of any drama.

> In judgements of art there are two elements, both of them
> forms of life that interact on each other. The work of art (in
> this case a play) is an expression of life by someone who has a
> point of view. It is not a mechanical object, like a refrigerator
> or a motor or a tractor. They can be judged by the efficiency
> with which they do the work they have been designed for. But a
> play is not static. It is incandescent; it radiates life.
> Not for everyone, however, or not for everyone in the same
> degree. Not everyone is attuned to the same wave length. For
> the observer is the second form of life in judgements of art,
> which represent an exchange of impulses between him and the
> art. The observer's opinion can be turned against him. It
> criticizes him as clearly as he criticizes art. What he thinks
> about the subject he is discussing discloses the baffling complex
> of his personality — his sensitive areas as well as the areas that
> are dead. Beauty is in the eye of the beholder, Emerson said.
> The man without beauty cannot see it.

Atkinson once wrote: 'Some day, somewhere, young people will
be thinking enviously of the time when Sean O'Casey was writing
mighty plays and Barry Fitzgerald and Sara Allgood were around

to act them.' To that statement one might add, 'and when Brooks
Atkinson was around to review them', because for nearly all
admirers of O'Casey, especially in the United States, the critic's
name was irrevocably linked with that of the playwright. No production of an O'Casey play in New York was complete without a
review from Atkinson; not only because his criticisms were in-
sightful, penetrating and perceptive, but also because the theatre
world knew that it was one friend writing about another friend,
and the warmth of that friendship was never absent from the
writing.

On the surface the friendship between Atkinson and O'Casey
was strange and unlikely. O'Casey also began his career as a
journalist, albeit an unpaid propagandist, but devoted no less to
the truth. Several of his political articles appeared in Irish jour-
nals up to 1913, the year of the great Dublin Lock-Out. That year
he threw himself into the trade union and socialist struggles, and
for several months in 1914 he wrote a regular column of 'Citizen
Army Notes' for the *Irish Worker*. In 1919 he published his first
book, *The Story of the Irish Citizen Army*, a pamphlet outlining
the developing of Dublin's militant workers' army. During this
time he was also writing plays, most of which were rejected by the
Abbey Theatre.

Atkinson, on the other hand, was from puritan New England.
A Harvard education and an appointment at Dartmouth were far
removed from O'Casey's proletarian, street education. And yet
that which they had in common — the drama — transcended
class barriers.

The two first met in the winter of 1934 when the playwright
came to New York to assist with the American premiere of *Within
the Gates*. (Their first formal contact had been in 1929 when
O'Casey, justifiably sensitive to any criticism of his rejected play,
The Silver Tassie, wrote to the critic and complained — 'very
courteously expressed', though — about one of Atkinson's
reviews.) O'Casey arrived at the docks aboard the *Majestic* on 19
September with £20 in his pocket, half of his life's savings, and
owing ten times as much. He was met by the dapper George Jean
Nathan, another of America's outstanding drama critics and a
champion of O'Casey's plays. While in New York, O'Casey stayed
at several hotels, including the Devon, from where he wrote
Atkinson a short note, thanking him for the kind reviews of *Within the Gates*, complimenting him on his prose and enclosing an

inscribed copy of *Windfalls* and a photo.

The meeting occurred one night when Nathan brought O'Casey to the Atkinsons' home on West 12th Street for dinner. True to form O'Casey showed up wearing his cap, coat and turtle neck sweater; the first time, Mrs Atkinson remembers, that anyone came to dinner in such garb. From all accounts it was a loud, noisy, boisterous and thoroughly enjoyable evening, though the Atkinsons' maid, outraged at the Irishman's dress, was left puzzled and bewildered by the antics of the company. That visit stuck in O'Casey's mind, for he mentioned it several times in subsequent letters to the critic. In 1937 he closed one letter by writing: 'And now, dear friend, farewell for the present, with remembrance of all your and your wife's kindness to me when I was in your City with its grand crown of a sky, and to dramatic critics, decent fellows because they never forgot to be human.'

To O'Casey, Atkinson had in him 'a love and respect for the drama', and he was a critic who was not swayed by the influence of others. In one respect he embodied O'Casey's romantic notion of America and her people: tough but fair-minded, a lover of the underdog, and blessed with an exciting dynamism. It was not so in Ireland or England, where O'Casey carried on running feuds with fellow dramatists and drama critics, and where, in Ireland at least, Yeats's influence was pervasive. To O'Casey, America was the home of Whitman, Emerson and Twain and of new and innovative things. It was a country on the move, growing in leaps and bounds. It was far different from England whose empire was rapidly disintegrating (a joy for O'Casey) and whose people seemed to be mired in an outmoded, obsolete class construct. Ireland, of course, was fast becoming a clerical state, and O'Casey had had enough of that in his forty-six years in Dublin.

Moreover, Atkinson, though known as a tough critic, was open to change in the drama, as all good critics must be. He was a leader in establishing the acceptance of new ideas, a role in harmony with O'Casey's criterion for a good critic. O'Casey once wrote to him: 'If a man is a dramatist then he must be in advance of his time; just as a man if he is a critic must be in advance of the drama of his time.'

Like most theatre observers Atkinson had a fondness for O'Casey's early plays, especially for *Juno and the Paycock* and *The Plough and the Stars*, which he considered the dramatist's finest works. In part this was due to the fact that not only were

they in and of themselves majestic plays, but Atkinson was fortunate to have seen them performed at their best and as they were
meant to be staged — by the Abbey Theatre players: Barry Fitzgerald and Sara Allgood, for whom the characters Captain and
Juno Boyle were created; F. J. McCormick, the indomitable
'Joxer'; Arthur Shields as Fluther Good; Sara Allgood again as
Bessie Burgess; and others like Eileen Crowe and Sydney Morgan.
Nothing Atkinson subsequently witnessed could equal those early
productions.

Unlike conventional critics, though, Atkinson championed
most of O'Casey's later plays. He saw excellent productions of
Within the Gates and *Red Roses for Me*, and performances of
Cock-a-Doodle Dandy, Purple Dust, and a few one-acters. But
like most of us he was handicapped by having only half a show —
the published text. He never saw a good production of *The Silver
Tassie* or any production of *The Star Turns Red, Oak Leaves and
Lavender* and O'Casey's plays of the 1950s. Nevertheless, he read
them and reviewed them and publicly wondered why O'Casey was
being neglected.

Yet, Atkinson was perceptive enough to know that O'Casey was
being ignored for several reasons. The dramatist's politics were
anathema to Cold War America. The entertainment industry
suffered a severe attack at the hands of the House of Un-Ameri-
can Activities Committee as federal agents probed the back-
grounds of producers, directors, actors and even stage hands,
looking for any communist 'tendencies'. A score of people were
blacklisted, and few were willing to risk their livelihood on
O'Casey's behalf.

Equally important, O'Casey's drama became increasingly difficult to perform. Atkinson wrote, 'Mr O'Casey has been free from
the disciplines of the stage. For an imaginative, eloquent, rebellious writer, this may not be a bad thing. But the more he is
divorced from the theatre the more he ignores the usually
accepted limitations of the stage. He lays enormous responsibility
on the director and the actors for translating his free-hand style
into theatrical terms.' Eric Bentley put it equally well: 'We don't
really know whether *Cock-a-Doodle Dandy* is good theatre, bad,
or indifferent, because we haven't tried it. ... Do we reject
O'Casey because as a communist he is beneath us or because as an
artist he is beyond us?'

To read the reviews of O'Casey by Atkinson is to review the

careers of both men. Only a year after Atkinson took over 'The Play' column, O'Casey's second published play, *Juno and the Paycock*, arrived in New York for its American premiere. In 1968, four years after the dramatist's death and a year before the critic retired, Atkinson wrote the last of his articles on O'Casey, a moving tribute and examination of the playwright's life. The change in both men between those years was one of growth, and it is reflected in the changes in Atkinson's two forms of life — the play and the observer.

ROBERT G. LOWERY

Part I

In Retrospect*

Thirteen days before Sean O'Casey died on 18 September 1964, at the age of eighty-four, a friend who was visiting him intercepted a telephone call. The call was from a London newspaperman who wanted to interview O'Casey. 'Tell him I'm talking only to God,' O'Casey replied with his familiar grin. When someone asked him on one of his last birthdays how he felt, he repeated something he had written about himself in his youth: 'Tired, but joyous, praising God for His rightness and the will towards joy in the hearts of men.'

Those remarks are interesting for two reasons. One: Although he described himself as a rationalist he was preoccupied with religion. His vocabulary was as rich in religious words and phrases as if he had been an evangelist. Two: He was an optimist about the human race. 'Merry', 'rejoice,' 'laughter,' 'dance,' 'song,' 'love' are words he used repeatedly. Since he was also cantankerous and petulant and since he struck out with terrible wrath against people and institutions that he regarded as harmful, it may seem arbitrary to describe him as a radiant man. The people he singled out for oblivion — W.H. Auden, Noel Coward, James Agate, Beverley Nichols, George Orwell, Denis Johnston, Kenneth Tynan — could hardly be expected to appreciate his radiance. Nor the Irish and British critics: he not only ran them down but he trampled on them repeatedly. In a large area of life he was contrary-minded and he wrote some very bitter prose.

But it was faith in life, love for his family and friends, and belief in a cheerful destiny that kept him going through a life of indigence and several personal catastrophes. He was affectionate, generous, and loyal towards those he loved and respected. His hatreds were confined to people and institutions that, in his opinion, impeded or impaired the normal joyousness of human existence. Among the advertising cards inside a Second Avenue

* From *The Sean O'Casey Reader*, edited and introduced by Brooks Atkinson (New York: St. Martin's Press, 1968).

bus in New York I was once surprised and delighted to find a quotation from O'Casey: 'I have found life an enjoyable, enchanting, active and sometimes terrifying experience, and I've enjoyed it completely. A lament in one ear, maybe, but always a song in the other.' This turned out to be a quotation from one of the hundreds of personal letters he wrote to hundreds of anonymous admirers, particularly in the United States, of which he was especially fond. O'Casey was a believer; it is a temptation to misuse a religious term and call him an Old Believer. That was his strength as a writer. 'The fire was in his hatred. The strength was in his love.'

He was a frail man, afflicted all his life with ulcerated eyes that resulted in almost total blindness in his last years. He suffered from lumbago that made movement painful; he had bronchial and respiratory troubles that consigned him to nursing homes repeatedly. But he left a prodigious body of exuberant work. Beginning at the age of thirty-eight, when his first writings were published (*Songs of the Wren* and *The Story of Thomas Ashe*) he wrote twelve full-length plays, fifteen one-act plays, six volumes of autobiography and four volumes of poems, short stories, reviews, articles and jeremiads. Although the literary forms changed, the basic point of view remained consistent.

He was born in a Dublin tenement on March 30, 1880, and baptized in a Protestant church as John Casey. Although the family was poor, his parents were cultivated people. Michael Casey, the father, was employed by a religious organization and had a big library that contained many religious books. When his son John was only six years old, Michael Casey died from injuries caused by a fall from a ladder he was using to reach the top shelf of his bookcases. The mother, Susan, was a woman of great sweetness and fortitude. She bore her husband thirteen children, only five of whom lived to be adults. Susan lived in tenements to the age of eighty without losing her kindness, pride, and inner grace. She appears throughout the first volume of O'Casey's autobiography, *I Knock at the Door*. There is a second sketch of her in the last volume, *Sunset and Evening Star*. She is also Mrs Breydon, the mother in *Red Roses for Me*, which is in many respects an autobiographical play.

Because of the painful disease in his eyes O'Casey could not attend school regularly. But throughout his long lifetime he had a passion for learning. In his youth he read widely in the classics and in the Bible. (At the age of eighty-four he was still learning by listening to the Schools Program of the British Broadcasting Corporation.) He went to work when he was an adolescent as a department store clerk, an experience entertainingly described in *Pictures in the Hallway*. Among his many random occupations was digging with pick and shovel. That was what he was doing when his first play, *Shadow of a Gunman*, was acted at the Abbey Theatre. (Total royalties from that production — £4.)

Although the family seems to have had middle-class standards of behavior, O'Casey was a natural rebel. He was never satisfied with the status quo. One of his early enthusiasms was the Gaelic language which was an important aspect of Irish nationalism. Caught up in the romantic hurly-burly of that cause, he gaeli-cized his name into Sean O'Cathasaigh, which he later simplified to O'Casey. When Jim Larkin led the long strike against the trolley monopoly in Dublin in 1913, O'Casey became an admirer and assistant. O'Casey was also thrilled by the Easter Rising against the British in 1916. He served for a time as secretary of the Irish Citizen Army and wrote articles supporting the cause. His early published writings derived from the labor movement and the rebellion. In addition to the *Songs of the Wren* and *The Story of Thomas Ashe*, who was a martyr to the movement, he wrote *The Story of the Citizen Army*, In his autobiography, written many years later, he said belonged to the world of discontent, resentment, and resistance.

But he had enough surplus energy to enjoy life even during the years when it was difficult to earn a bare living. He wrote and sang songs in an appealing Irish voice. As a youth he sang hymns in church with an enthusiasm that left an impression on other churchgoers; and when the moment for voluntary prayers came he could be counted on for one that was long and fervent. At the age of ten he rehearsed Shakespeare with his brother, who was an amateur actor; and at fifteen he played Henry VI in an amateur production on the stage that later became the Abbey Theatre. He also played in Boucicault's *The Shaughraun* in a professional cast in which he replaced a regular actor.

Using odd sheets of paper of different sizes that he picked up here and there and ink that he made, he also wrote three plays that he submitted to the Abbey. They were all rejected. But they compelled the Abbey management to take an interest in this strange workman with an independent point of view. O'Casey had attended performances at the Abbey only twice, once to see Shaw's *Androcles and the Lion*. 'Not far from being a good play,' the Abbey management said about the first one that O'Casey had submitted. Lady Gregory, a wonderful woman who was one of O'Casey's three heroines (his mother and his wife being the other two), told him after reading his third play: 'I believe there is something in you, and your strong point is characterisation.' If it had not been for W. B. Yeats, who was the most powerful voice in the council, the Abbey might have produced the third play, which was called *The Crimson and the Tri-Color*.

O'Casey's fourth play, *Shadow of a Gunman*, was produced by the Abbey in 1923 when O'Casey was forty-three years of age and supporting himself as a common laborer. The next play, produced in 1924, was *Juno and the Paycock*, which is a world classic; and the third was produced in 1926, *The Plough and the Stars*, also a classic and, in my opinion, O'Casey's finest play. Those two roaring plays are steeped in the Irish tenement life that O'Casey had known intimately all his life with its poverty, irresponsibility, temperament, kindness, treachery and civil war; the characters exude vitality, and the dialogue is racy, pungent, and comic. Certain phrases from *Juno and the Paycock* have become part of our literary currency — Captain Boyle's repeated remark that 'the whole world's in a terrible state of chassis', and Joxer's shiftless adjective 'darlin',' as in 'A darlin' funeral, a daarlin' funeral' or 'a darlin' song, a daarlin' song.' Mrs Tancred's scream of agony is another famous and piercing speech: 'Sacred Heart o' the Crucified Jesus, take away our hearts o' stone . . . and give us hearts o' flesh! . . . Take away this murdherin' hate . . . an' give us Thine eternal love!'

When those two plays were first produced and were acted also in other parts of the world O'Casey became famous and successful. Although he continued writing for thirty-five years, none of his later plays had the impact of those two. Eventually he came to resent the fact that he was most widely known as the author of those two early plays, and many years later he said that they would survive only as historical documents and that *Cock-a-Doodle Dandy*, written in 1949 when he was sixty-nine years old, was his best play. Despite the variety, vitality, high aspirations and originality of most of the later plays, *Juno and the Paycock* and *The Plough and the Stars* in my opinion retain the highest rank because of the comic extravagance of the dialogue, the mercurial temperament of the characters, and the earthiness of the themes. The plays leaped fresh out of O'Casey's daily experience. Given the liveliness of his own personality, he could never be dull or prosaic. But when he left Ireland in self-imposed exile in 1926 he left the environment that had fed his mind and stimulated his spirit for forty-six years. He also left a band of Irish actors whose speech and gusto have not been equaled. For the rest of his professional life O'Casey needed actors as exuberant as Arthur Sinclair, Barry Fitzgerald, F. J. McCormick, Arthur Shields, Maire O'Neill, Sara Allgood, Eileen Crowe and the other lively members of that matchless company. When O'Casey was writing his later plays — particularly *Cock-a-Doodle Dandy* — it seems to me that he was still hearing in his mind those lilting voices that could transmute temperamental remarks into explosive comedy or tragedy. If most of the later plays are difficult to act, it is because that unique band of actors is no longer in existence.

O'Casey had created an unhackneyed and non-academic style of theatre. From reading Shakespeare, from acting in Boucicault and, let us not forget, out of his own vivid talent, he had learned how to combine comedy and tragedy into a single instrument. 'I tell you, life is not one thing but many things, a wide branching flame, grand and good to see, dazzling to the eye of no-one loving it,' says Ayamonn in the autobiographical *Red Roses for Me*. Some traditionalists, like T. S. Eliot, regarded O'Casey's intuitive style as an impure art form of which they disapproved. Some complained that the plays were so diffuse that they could not understand what O'Casey was getting at or on which side he stood. All his life he was condescended to by traditional academicians. But theatregoers all over the world have never had any difficulty in understanding and appreciating *Juno and the Paycock* and *The Plough and the Stars*, which are intensifications of experience and part of the vernacular of the theatre.

In 1928 O'Casey wrote *The Silver Tassie*. Nothing was the same for him after that. Labeled a tragi-comedy, it is a play about the price the common people have to pay for the cruelty and stupidity of war. Of the four acts three continue the familiar liveliness of the O'Casey style. The second act is a sketch of battlefields written in the expressionistic style of chants and dance movement. Since *Juno and the Paycock* and *The Plough and the Stars* saved the Abbey Theatre from bankruptcy, O'Casey had a right to expect the Abbey to stage his next play. But it did not. In an insufferably patronizing and belittling letter, Yeats said among other things: 'You have no subject. You are not interested in the Great War.'

Instead of accepting the rejection humbly, O'Casey turned it into a public scandal that must have been as traumatic an experience for Yeats and the Abbey Theatre council as the rejection had been for him. He always had a talent for making sensational exits on high moral principles. He had resigned from the Council of the Irish Citizen Army when a vote went against him. He emigrated from Ireland in the mood of a martyr; on that occasion he said of himself: 'He was a voluntary and settled exile from every creed, from every party and from every literary clique.' Now he made reconciliation with the Abbey impossible by the vehemence of his rebuke to Yeats. But it seems to me that he was well justified in rejecting Yeats' pompous comments. *The Silver Tassie* is an original drama on an enlightened theme, and its point of view is civilized and humane. Bernard Shaw thought highly of *The Silver Tassie*: 'What a hell of a play!' he exclaimed enthusiastically. After seeing the London production the next year, Lady Gregory wrote in her journal: 'I am convinced we ought to have taken it and done our best to put it on and make such cuts of the bad language as he would allow.' Yeats later admitted that the rejection was a mistake. *The Silver Tassie* states forcefully the evangelical point of view that became the basic theme of the rest of O'Casey's life.

In his next play, *Within the Gates* (1933), he took the deep plunge into a dramatic form that was the equivalent of allegory — part dance, part song, nearer to ballet and music than to the simpler form of his early plays. Now he was trying to deal less with people than with philosophical essences. 'The closer we approach to actual life, the further we move away from the drama,' he wrote in 1934 when *Within the Gates* was acted in New York. 'If a play is what it ought to be it must be a religious function, whether it is played before a community of thousands or a community of ten.' Although *Within the Gates* sets the theatre some serious problems in staging, it is worth the effort. There is an abundance of mercy and compassion in this complex morality play, as illustrated by the poignant character of the Bishop. What the Bishop learns about life is tender and humiliating. Although *Within the Gates* has a pagan exterior, it has a religious code of values.

O'Casey is against cant, sanctimoniousness, arbitrariness, and everything that diminishes the energy and scope of life — everything that inhibits 'dancing in the gold and purple pavilions of laburnum and lilac' which represented the beauty of life to him.

Red Roses for Me (published in 1942; produced in 1943) is a beautifully written drama with interpolated songs and dances that in large part tells O'Casey's own story in terms of romantic tragedy. *Purple Dust* (published in 1940; produced in 1944) is one of his most popular plays. It makes satiric comedy out of the loutishness of Irish peasants and the superciliousness of some wealthy Britishers. Since the form is simple, this play is easy to act.

Cock-a-Doodle Dandy is the best constructed of the plays written in a fantastic style. Against a background of quarrelsome Irish men, impulsive Irish women and the inevitable parish priest with his obsequious followers, O'Casey created the mythic figure of the Cock to represent the joyful spirit of life and to draw an invidious comparison with the avarice, fears, superstition and callousness of human beings. When it was produced in London in 1959, an English theatre critic wrote some admiring comments: 'A rollicking fantasy that burns with compassion and crackles with wit.' In both form and theme it represents the tremendous vitality of O'Casey's spirit and his unequaled gift for shining language. I saw this play in a production that could not express the buoyancy and the virtuosity of the script. But *Cock-a-Doodle Dandy* need not remain a victim of the theatre's literal-mindedness. Some director with access to a first-rate acting company (as Peter Brooke had in the British company that played *Marat/de Sade*) could make something gay and glorious out of this text. It has certain deficiencies. In comparison with *Juno and the Paycock* and *The Plough and the Stars* it shows O'Casey's increasing preoccupation with ideas rather than people. He was becoming the teacher instead of the poet. The characters are symbols rather than people. But in view of the literary vitality, humane principle, and melodious language of the play, the burden of proof is on the theatre. Although the comedians of the Abbey Theatre are no longer in existence, some troupe ought to be able to act *Cock-a-Doodle Dany* eloquently.

O'Casey wrote two more full length plays — *The Bishop's Bonfire* (produced in 1955), and *The Drums of Father Ned* (produced in 1959). *The Bishop's Bonfire* makes rowdy comedy out of the loutishness of some Irish people after the style of *Purple Dust*. Published under the rubric of 'A Sad Play Within the Tune of a Polka,' it lampoons the stuffiness of formal religion. When it was produced in Dublin at the Gaiety Theatre it extracted more venom than usual from the Dublin critics and disturbed some members of the audience. But it was a solid success that showed how much interest the Irish people still took in their pugnacious emigré who invariably gave them a good thumping. O'Casey's whooping rejoinder to the outcries of the Irish critics appears in this book.

The Drums of Father Ned, which O'Casey described as 'This comedy's but an idle, laughing play/About things encumbering Ireland's way,' became as much a cause célèbre as *The Silver Tassie*, although for a different reason. It was to have been part of the Dublin International Theatre Festival during the Tostal celebration of 1958; a play made from Joyce's *Ulysses* was to have been a companion piece. But several months before the festival was to open, the Archbishop of Dublin announced that he would not perform the Votive Mass if plays by O'Casey and Joyce were to be acted. Since this was tantamount to a boycott of the Tostal by the most powerful man in Dublin, the Council hastily rejected *The Drums of Father Ned*, as well as *Ulysses*. Not to be outdone by a bishop, O'Casey put a resounding ban on further performances of his plays in Ireland — on the stage or radio. He could hurl a thunderbolt as fiercely as anyone.

The Drums of Father Ned would have been particularly appropriate because it makes comedy out of some harum-scarum antics at a Tostal festival. Father Ned, who does not appear in the play, beats a drum in support of a more joyous Ireland than Church or state permit. The young people, in whom O'Casey always had a mystic faith, take the festival away from their cautious elders and put their hearts and shoulders into feats of merriment. 'Lassies an' lads, it's time to go, for more life, more laughter, a sturdier spirit and a stronger heart,' says the mayor's exuberant though incorrigible son. 'Father Ned is on the march.'

In addition to the full-length plays O'Casey wrote fifteen one-act plays. He discarded the earliest one-acts from his collected works; presumably he did not regard them as up to the standard to which he aspired. Many of the one-acts are knock-about pieces like the small plays that used to be called 'curtain-raisers'. They are examples of O'Casey's fondness for the hearty laugh of theatrical enjoyment. In 1961, when he was eighty-one years of age, he published three short plays under the title of the first play — *Behind the Green Curtains*. Written in three scenes, *Behind the Green Curtains* is another broadside attack on the joylessness of Ireland under the thumbs of the Church and religious bigots. 'Catholics, Protestants and you unbelievers seem to be frightened fools,' says the most generous-hearted woman in the play.

The second play, *Figuro in the Night*, is a harlequinade directed at what O'Casey calls 'The Ferocious Chastity of Ireland,' — entertaining to read, difficult to stage. *The Moon Shines on Kylenamoe* is a one-act skit that contrasts the self-assurance of a British bureaucrat with the suspicion, animosity, and malice of some Irish country people.

All these three last plays convey the wholesomeness of O'Casey's mind, the ingenuity of his imagination, and the brightness of his spirit. Although they lack the sustained mockery of *Bedtime Story*, they express the extraordinary grace of his old age. His eyesight was fading so fast that he had to be read to and his health was infirm. But the spirit that began in a Dublin tenement remained indomitable.

I have left to the last my comments on O'Casey's only humorless play — *The Star Turns Red*, which was put on by a left-wing group in London in 1940. It was O'Casey's salute to Communism. From an artistic point of view it is dogmatic and sterile, like most party-line plays. But it has one significant factor: again there are religious undertones, or so it seems to me: 'The star turned red is still the star of him who came as a man's pure prince of peace,' says one of the characters in the last act of this apocalyptic play. O'Casey's Communism should be discussed because it was just about as original in form as *Within the Gates* or *Cock-a-Doodle Dandy*. There was less of political Communism in it than O'Casey's personal rebelliousness and humanitarianism. Jesus was a Communist, by O'Casey's standards. In his opinion Keats, Shelley, and Dickens were Communists; so was Whitman, and just about anyone he admired. 'Any man who is honest and gives all he can to the community is a Communist,' O'Casey said. When his children were growing up he once remarked to me: 'I am not trying to convert them to Communism. I don't think anyone has the right to try to control the minds of his children. I urge them to make up their own minds. But, of course, I'm hoping that they will turn out to be Communists.'

Since he made this comment during one of the most frigid moments of the Cold War when Great Britain and the United States were almost hysterically anti-Communist, the remark seemed to me comically eccentric. Because I could never take his Communism seriously, I wondered if his children could, since they represent a skeptical generation. I asked his daughter, Shivaun, what she thought. His Communism did not seem eccentric to her. 'Sean was a humanitarian, a Communist and a pure spirit,' she replied. 'He saw a long way into the future and saw things improving all the time. . . . I miss talking to him now; it seems as if a great piece of life and knowledge has gone.' She added that 'he knew very well what was happening in Russia and China, and saw that his ideals were being arrived at quicker there than in other countries, particularly the capitalistic ones.' In O'Casey's home, familiarity bred love and devotion.

But I am a member of the skeptical generation on this issue. O'Casey was never a member of the Communist Party. I think his non-membership in a party he actively supported was significant. It indicated not only his fundamental independence, but also his congenital distrust of any organization that required so much discipline, whether it was a political party or the Roman Catholic Church. He was incapable of accepting discipline from any external source. There is not much about Lenin or Stalin in his comments on Communism.

Never a man to do anything by halves, he supported Communism uncritically. He wrote articles for the London *Daily Worker* until his eyesight made it necessary to reduce his writing commitments. Although he never went to Moscow he proclaimed it his Holy City with the jubilance of a convert. He paid homage to Moscow as 'a flame to light the way of all men towards the people's ownership of the earth; where revolution stands in man's holy fire, and in the rich mosaic of a red wall.' In what he wrote for the *New Times* in Moscow his style could be uncharacteristically humble; he accepted Communist propaganda as reality. He denied that there was censorship in Russia because, as he pointed out, it was not mentioned in the 'History of the Communist Party.' He grandly dismissed as a bore a disillusioned British woman who told him that when she and her husband were working in some Commissariat in Moscow her husband was picked up by the OGPU and disappeared permanently. O'Casey concluded that probably her husband had taken this portentous way of escaping from a wife he couldn't stand any longer.

After *The Star Turns Red* O'Casey never wrote another propaganda play, although there is a self-righteous Communist in *Oak Leaves and Lavender*, which is otherwise an amusing play about some of the crotchets of the home life of England during World War II. With the exception of *The Star Turns Red* and *Oak Leaves and Lavender*, it seems to me that O'Casey abided by his own philosophy: 'As a man the revolutionist playwright is much the same as the drama critic: he has to get better from an illness by sending for a doctor; his personal problems cannot be solved by a constant reading of the Communist Manifesto; so when he's writing a play, the dramatist is neither Tory nor Communist, but only a playwright, setting down his characters as he knew them, giving, if he can, added depth, height and lilt to the words he makes them speak.'

O'Casey's Communism had a flamboyant style. But it must have perplexed orthodox Communists. As usual, he made his own rules and preserved his personal independence.

In 1939, when he and his family were living in Totnes, Devon, and he was still writing plays, O'Casey published the first volume of his autobiography, *I Knock at the Door*, which chronicled the first ten years of his life in Dublin. It is a masterpiece of recollection, mood, perception and writing. Before he finished the autobiography in 1954, he had written six volumes. In *Sean O'Casey, the Man and His Work*, which is the best book on the subject, David Krause has described the time spans of the various volumes as follow: '*I Knock at the Door* (1939) 1880–1890; *Pictures in the Hallway* (1942) 1891–1904; *Drums under the Windows* (1946) 1905–1916; *Inishfallen, Fare Thee Well* (1949) 1916–1926; *Rose and Crown* (1952) 1926–1934; *Sunset and Evening Star* (1954) 1934–1953. In 1956 the six volumes were collected in two volumes and published under the generic title of *Mirror in My House*.

The autobiographies are not an orderly record of O'Casey's life, complete with names, dates, and records. They are offered as a conscious work of art. O'Casey tells the story of his life in terms of a grand myth, like Joyce's *Ulysses*, and, in some elusive manner, the Old Testament, as if his own life were a footnote to the mythology of mankind, part of the 'sad, sweet silent music of humanity.' In the early volumes the chief character is called

Casside, but he becomes Sean O'Casside in the third
and finally Sean O'Casey. The chronology is often confusing. The author repeatedly returns to scenes that he has left,
or he anticipates other scenes without explanation. He is concerned, not with facts, but with the vicissitudes and wonders of
life.

Although the autobiographies are primarily concerned with
basic subjects, like children, homes, schools, debts, people, pubs,
theatres, history, they are written in a key of high emotion by a
man caught up in the ecstasy of words — long, rushing sentences
that describe a wide range of human experience. The point of
view is detached, as if the volumes were fiction, but the style is
overwhelmingly personal. Some of it is fantastically comic; some
of it is fiercely proud; some of it explodes with anger. It is also, I
think, a lonely book by a man separated from the centers of
activity and recalling with nostalgia things that happened long
ago.

The first two volumes of the autobiographies have been very
successfully recast into the form of stage readings by Paul Shyre,
an American admirer of O'Casey, and brilliantly staged by Stuart
Vaughan. Sitting behind lecterns on plain stages, some of the
most talented American actors have on several occasions created
memorable evenings by reading sections of *I Knock at the Door*
and *Pictures in the Hallway*. Arranged in a simple, classical form,
the stage readings have turned out to be tender and comic in the
best style of O'Casey. The autobiographies are also the basic
material from which a film about O'Casey, *Young Cassidy*, was
made in 1965. Since the part of O'Casey was acted by a vigorous,
swashbuckling young man, Rod Taylor, the film did not have
much literal resemblance to the autobiographies.

As Mrs Gogan says in *The Plough and the Stars*: 'There's
always the makin's of a row in th' mention of religion,' and religion keeps cropping up throughout the autobiographies. Men of
the cloth receive a lot of attention — the Reverend E. M. Griffin,
whom O'Casey revered second only to his mother in his youth and
whose photograph is the frontispiece to the third volume; also, Dr
Michael O'Hickey and Dr Walter McDonald, both of whom
defied their ecclesiastical superiors on matters of principle and in
the O'Casey lexicon became martyrs. Only a religious man who
had lost the innocence of his youthful faith could take such an
evangelical interest in religion as O'Casey did. It is, incidentally,

significant that he dedicated *The Drums of Father Ned* to the memories of five priests, all of whom defied the Church in some act of insubordination. O'Casey admired them. Gestures of defiance usually won O'Casey's approval. He was a veteran in that field.

In his last years Sean O'Casey was a thin man, with sharp features, lusterless eyes, a fighting jaw, an entracing Irish voice and a gay spirit. He lived a warm and intimate family life in the third-floor flat of a house on a hill in Torquay, Devon. Although the flat was small it was brightly decorated. Perhaps because of his impaired vision, he liked brilliant colors, and took particular pleasure in the decoration of all the places where he lived, including his room in the Dublin tenement. The bright colors extended to his dress. When Shivaun was eight years old she made a gaily-colored cap or 'beanie' from him at school — yellow, red, and navy blue. Since the cap kept O'Casey's head warm in winter he continued to wear it. Shivaun made him three or four more, and then people all over the world sent him so many bizarrely decorated caps that he soon had a large collection and could choose a cap to fit his mood every day. Out of a Mexican blanket, Shivaun also made him a red house coat that he wore in the cold weather. He had always worn jerseys and sweaters, but when he married, Eileen introduced him to the turtle-necked sweater, which became the badge of his tribe — the working man. As he stumbled cautiously around the flat, smoking Erinmore tobacco in a battered pipe, he looked like a cross between a chief rabbi and a giddy bishop.

To say that he was fortunate in his family life would be to imply that he was not primarily responsible for it. But he was. Family came first in his order of values. In 1927 when he was forty-seven years of age, he married Eileen Reynolds Carey, who was then in her early twenties and was playing Nora in a London production of *The Plough and the Stars*. He was or had been a Protestant; she was a Catholic, and they were married by a Catholic priest. His marriage was about the best thing that ever happened to him. When they married he was famous as author of *Juno and the Paycock* and *The Plough and the Stars*. He had reason to assume that the rest of his life would be equally exciting and profitable, and his bride was also well established in her own right as an actress. She lived in a comfortable flat of her own.

Their life did not turn out to be as bountiful as they probably expected. They had hardly married before the angry controversy over *The Silver Tassie* broke out, and O'Casey was in serious financial trouble almost at once. But Eileen, an attractive woman with great strength and force of character, was equal to every crisis the family had to cope with for the rest of their lives. They had three children — Breon, born in 1928, Niall, born in 1936 (died in 1956) and Shivaun, born in 1939. If O'Casey and his wife had been complaisant people they could probably have organised a secure professional life in the theatre world of London. Both of them were talented and well known. But after a few years of moving from one flat to another they left London and settled down in Totnes, Devon, to be near Dartington Hall School where the children were educated. Children outranked career in the family code of values.

During these years when he was writing plays and his autobiographies he also wrote innumerable essays, articles, stories and poems which are collected in four of his most caustic volumes: *The Flying Wasp* (1937), *The Green Crow* (1956), *Under a Colored Cap* (1963) and *Blasts and Benedictions* (1967, posthumous). In *The Green Crow* he observed that some Latin writer once said that 'If a crow could feed in quiet, it would have more meat.' He added that he, who came to be known as the Green Crow, would doubtless have had more meat if he had kept his 'big beak shut.' But he could never back away from a fight. The words, the epithets, the derision flew in all directions, and most people ran for cover.

The frontispiece of the original edition of *Pictures in the Hallway* consists of a studio photograph of O'Casey in his twenties. Neatly attired in gray trousers and a dark vest and jacket, his hands in his trouser pockets, the pugnacious Gaelic Leaguer lounges on a carved studio table and takes a cocky look into the eye of the camera. Very grand; very sure of himself; everything is there except the humor, which made all the difference between a bore and a great humanitarian. The frontispiece of the original edition of *The Bishop's Bonfire* is a black-and-white reproduction of Breon O'Casey's painting of his father. In his old age, under a capacious round field hat, holding an open book in his left hand, O'Casey has the stern look of a reproachful prophet. Again, the humor is missing. But the humor is of fundamental importance. Humor indicates an acceptance of the imperfection of life;

humor is the adjustment to human realities. All his life O'Casey professed to be surprised when people took exception to his fulminations. For he was personally a modest man. His attitude towards life and his conception of his place in it are well expressed in a letter he wrote to Harold Macmillan, his friend and publisher, in 1951:

> I cannot expect, nor do I expect, that everyone should like and agree with my 'judgment.' I don't think 'judgment' to be right word about what I state or seem to imply in play or biography. They are opinions only; honest ones, taken after thought and long and wide experience of men and things; but they are, for all that, far from being infallible. Only God or Time can vindicate the judgment of man. To me one thing alone is certain — we are all one in the tremendous and glorious bond of humanity. Jew, Gentile, bond and free, Tory and Communist can never break away from this grand bond. We are born, we die and we must do the best we can between the day of birth and the night of death.

When he reached his eighties his vision had deteriorated so rapidly that he could see nothing except the difference between light and dark. 'All the hundreds of books around me are dumb,' he said, though without self-pity. Now he was totally dependent on others to read to him; and chiefly on Eileen, who was everything to him, even more than she had been before. The width of his life contracted accordingly. In better days they had read the London *Daily Worker* and *The Times* of London every day, and frequently the *Manchester Guardian,* and they had subscribed to two Irish newspapers. When he could no longer read they reduced the daily newspapers to *The Times* and one Dublin paper. Those were all Eileen had time to read in addition to parts of books and articles in periodicals that contained things he wanted to know about. He depended on the radio for daily news.

But he never surrendered. He remembered that Beethoven wrote his greatest symphonies when he was deaf; that Prescott was half-blind when he wrote *History of the Conquest of Mexico* and that Renoir went on painting when he was so rheumatic that he had to tie the brush to his hand. O'Casey kept on learning about music and other things by listening to instructive programs on BBC radio. He never considered himself too old to be instructed about anything from any source. Although he had plenty of pride he was never too proud to learn something new. As he went swirling (his word) around the streets of the St Marychurch part of Torquay, the beauties and complexities of life astounded him. It seemed to him that life was so fantastic that writers and artists did not need to invent anything more remarkable.

A little less than a month before he died he wrote a mocking condemnation of the theatre of cruelty under the sardonic title 'The Bald Primaqueera,' which was a parody of the title of Eugène Ionesco's *The Bald Prima Donna*. The prose style of O'Casey's epilogue is a little labored, as if he were pushing himself just beyond his strength; the style does not have the reverberant energy of 'Bonfire Under a Black Sun'. But his faith in life is as sweet and exultant as ever. Still hating the nay-sayers, he still believes in the basic goodness of humanity. He continues to translate everything and everybody out of the tiny particular into the grand mythology of life which he still loved and revered.

Over the forty-six years of his literary career the quality of his writing was uneven. Although he wrote the most glorious English of his era — the English nearest in color and strength to the Elizabethan — the content did not always support the imagery. But he was creative and imaginative and he was spiritually alive until the last moment. He had the moral courage of an idealist. Whatever his religious ideas may have been, I think God had reason to be proud of Sean O'Casey.

Part II
The Plays

Irish Folk Life in a Tragedy*

JUNO AND THE PAYCOCK, A PLAY IN THREE ACTS BY SEAN O'CASEY

Comedy of Irish character and tragedy of Irish political life, in fairly equal parts comprise the substance of Sean O'Casey's *Juno and the Paycock*, put on last evening at the Mayfair Theatre.[1] Surely both those elements convey the full quality of the Dublin life four years ago represented by Mr O'Casey's drama. To join them as bluntly as Mr O'Casey has done, however, and to require at the same time an even performance, is to throw rather too much responsibility upon the director. In the current version the tragic moments come off vigorously, expressing genuine pathos seasoned with pure theatre; but although the two principal comic roles are enacted pungently by Augustin Duncan and Claude Cooper, the comedy scenes in general need considerable molding and polishing. Accordingly, one of the most understanding plays of the season, full of folk-life and written with a sense of the theatre, becomes uneven and scattered in the playing.

Most of the theatrical news from Ireland of late has brought frequent report of Mr O'Casey's remarkable success at the Abbey Theatre, and on the simultaneous rejuvenation of that familiar institution. No doubt, the essential, conclusive proof of the strength of his talent was the reception of his current piece there, *The Plough and the Stars*.[2] On the first night the actors were mobbed; only the intervention of the 'polis' (whose characters are sadly blackened in *Juno*) made the continuance of the performance possible. Perhaps that new tragedy comes even closer home to Dubliners today than *Juno and the Paycock*. But after two acts of volatile character comedy, the final scenes of *Juno* are grim enough, pointed enough as well, with their quick revenge for the treacherous murder of a comrade. With pistols drawn, two 'irregulars' hustle off Johnny Boyle, already half-dead in the

* *The New York Times* (16 Mar. 1926).

27

service of his country, and word soon comes of his murder in a
dark corner of the city.

Thus Mr O'Casey twists the dagger he has already plunged
deep into the life of the Boyle family. For just previously the
legacy they had been anticipating rather jauntily had been
denied them, and Mary's gentlemanly lover had left her with
child. 'Ah, what can God do agen the stupidity of men!' exclaims
Juno in despair. In the accumulation of tragedy, as well in his
treatment of an incident, Mr O'Casey cannot let well enough
alone. However skilfully he may have designed this play, he has
overwritten nearly every point.

In spite of the fact that the second act in particular expands the
comedy of character far beyond its dramatic value, these folk
scenes reveal Mr O'Casey at his best. Not only does he understand
the child-like people of whom he is writing here, and sympathize
with their points of view, but he also conveys his knowledge
through brilliant colloquial dialogue. Part of the flavor of these
character scenes is diffused in the current performance by an
enervating pace in the acting, and by different conceptions in the
creation of the parts. But the scenes portraying the bragging,
shiftless 'Captain' Jack Boyle and his 'artful dodger' satellite
abound in gracious, objective humor. For although this lazy head
of the family speaks bold and brave words when only the cautious
'Joxer' is present to echo approval, he quavers before the sharp
tongue of his wife.

Upon Juno, wife of the gay, cavalier 'Captain,' falls all the responsibility of the household. While he drinks with his comrade
in the corner 'snug,' and feels sharp pains in his legs whenever a
job looms menacingly on the horizon, she keeps the family in
operation, cajoles the green-grocer, cares for her shattered son,
protects her daughter when every one else turns against her, and
pushes her husband into the moleskin trousers for service on the
new job. According to the device of Mr O'Casey's drama, the gods
intervene just in time. Just as the 'Captain' seems fated to descend
into honest toil, Charlie Bentham appears with news of a legacy.
The new turn in the Boyle fortunes gives rise to the jollification of
the second act amid all the new furniture, the 'jars' full of merriment, the singing of ballads, and 'Joxer's' short-memoried attempts at tuneful 'renditions.'

And the 'Captain's' solemn flights at conversation, his manly
talk of the decline in Consols, the meddling of the Church in

affairs of the nation, and his invariable conclusion: 'I tell yer, the whole world's in a turrible state o' chassis!' After the sudden tragedy in the final act, after Juno has gone off to see her murdered son and Mary has deserted the barren household, the play ends on this note of folk-comedy with the 'Captain' and Joxer back from the barroom, their skins full and their lips heavy with philosophy.

Like the direction, the acting is uneven. Mr Duncan and Mr Cooper do well with their two roles, and make for amusing contrast. As Juno, Miss Randolph likewise creates a character in the round without laying on thick the tragedy in the end. Mr Macollum stresses too violently his voice and his gestures as Johnny Boyle. Miss Hill is difficult to understand in the part of Mary. As a voluble neighbor, Miss Daniels is merry and pleasing. Mr Cullinan's brief appearance as a thrifty tailor reveals a certain strength of character. As Mrs Tancred Miss McComb is thoroughly competent. But like the play itself, the serviceability of several of the character portraits is endangered by the slow pace of the performance. Instead of being caught up in the illusion, one has time to see the reverse side of the acting.

NOTES

1. Produced by H.W. Romberg in association with John Jay School at the Mayfair Theatre, 15 March 1926. Total performances: 74.

Cast:		
	Captain Jack Boyle	Augustin Duncan
	Juno Boyle	Louise Randolph
	Johnny Boyle	Barry Macollum
	Mary Boyle	Isabel Stuart Hill
	'Joxer' Daly	Claude Cooper
	Mrs Maisie Madigan	Eleanor Daniels
	'Needle' Nugent	Ralph Cullinan
	Mrs Tancred	Kate McComb
	A Neighbor	Mildred McCoy
	Jerry Devine	Lewis Martin
	Charlie Bentham	Charles Webster
	An Irregular Mobilizer	J. Augustus Keogh
	An Irregular	Wallace House
	A Coal Block Vendor	Emmet O'Reilly
	A Furniture Removal Man	G.O. Taylor
	A Sewing Machine Man	G.O. Taylor
	Helper	Emmet O'Reilly

Staged by Augustin Duncan

miere, 8 February 1926, Abbey Theatre. Riots broke out on the
fourth nights of the play.

O'Casey at the Bat*

JUNO AND THE PAYCOCK: HIS FIRST AMERICAN PRODUCTION

Something of the warm, cordial character of Irish people informs
Sean O'Casey's *Juno and the Paycock*, now at the Mayfair
Theatre.[1] And in Irish matters, which take such effective prece-
dence over pure reason, the glowing warmth of the Irish temperament becomes the charm and the only viable constant. When
George Moore, pallid grandee of Ebury Street, returned to Ireland after sniffing the art of Paris and London, he made a similar
observation: 'I've noticed,' he said to a young friend, 'even within
the few days I have been in Ireland, that Ireland is spoken of not
as a geographical but a sort of human entity.' Mr Moore picks up
things very rapidly.

For Dubliners, Mr O'Casey's tragedy (which might be a comedy
quite as logically) doubtless has immediate significance for its
reflection of the terrors and horrors through which the Free State
was born. After two acts of volatile characterization, quite disarming by reasons of its humor, fidelity and magnetic hospitality,
Johnny Boyle is slain in cold blood by the irregulars, seemingly a
gratuitous end to a life already half given in his country's service.
'Oh, it's thrue,' his sister moans, 'It's thrue what Jerry Devine says
— there isn't a God, there isn't a God; it there was He wouldn't let
these things happen.' It is terrible because it seems so futile. And
it is terrible in Mr O'Casey's drama because by the skill of construction he gives his audience only the most casual warning. After
several uncommonly ruddy scenes inside the Boyle home, scenes
of domestic tribulation, comic skullduggery and unalloyed
human nature, the inexorable revenge of the political warriors
falls suddenly, like the stroke of the headsman's axe. And the

* *New York Times* (21 Mar. 1926).

Boyle family, already on the brink of disaster, immediately dis-
integrates. Thus, Mr O'Casey, with all-consuming pity for his
country, brings the affairs of the nation brutally across the thres-
hold into the home where all the finer qualities of life may
flourish. Small wonder that this drama, and a similar one, *The
Plough and the Stars*, just produced, found a quick response in
Dublin. 'Ah, what can God do agen the stupidity o' man!'
exclaims Mrs Boyle, whose husband and son give her small con-
solation. And for opposite reasons.

For her husband is merely the roving, childlike, good-for-
nothing loafer of comedy in general. With the chicken-livered
Joxer ever at his heels, ready to drink and sing whenever the
'missus' is not at home, 'Captain' Jack Boyle leads a glorious and
shiftless existence — 'lookin' for work,' as Joxer remarks, 'an'
prayin' to God he won't get it!' When work turns up, when Father
Farrell sends word of a job, 'that's goin' on in Rathmines,' and
Mrs Boyle commands him to put on his moleskin trousers and to
'get along,' pains begin to twinge in the old man's barometric
legs. 'Nobody but meself knows the sufferin' I'm goin' through
with the pains in these legs o' mine!' In the consideration of such
simple-minded folk all the usual laws of thrift and industriousness
go wide of their mark; only intelligent people, with a strong sense
of responsibility, suffer through unemployment. After all his sub-
terfuges have failed Boyle almost starts out toward Rathmines
when the good God intervenes with news of a legacy. Such a
transformation! Immediately Boyle swells with good intentions.
'I'll never doubt the goodness o' God agen,' he says devoutly.
Away with the trifling Joxer!

> He'll never blow the truth off a pint o' mine agen, that's a sure
> thing. Johnny . . . Mary . . . you're to keep yourselves to your-
> selves for the future. Juno, I'm done with Joxer . . . I'm a new
> man from this out. . . (*Clasping Juno's hand, and singing
> emotionally*):
>   Oh, me darlin' Juno, I will be thrue to thee:
>   Me own, me darlin' Juno, you're all the world to me.

Mr O'Casey has seasoned his second act with the pungent flavor
of high-spirited characterization. If the childlike qualities of his
people ever appear completely ingenuous, this second act of pure
social exuberance gives them free play. Even the sharp-tongued

Juno, the real anchor of the Boyle family, buries her complaints and responsibilities. Drinking, singing, dancing catch up the entire Boyle menage in a whirl of happy celebration, welcome Joxer back, swallow the voluble Mrs Madigan and almost capti-vate the intellectually snobbish Bentham. Here we have the poetry, the gregariousness, the ebullience, credulity and general warm-heartedness of the Irish people. Even the stiff-legged 'Captain' Boyle, well soaked in whisky, steps a few maudlin poetic meters — uncertainly. 'Give us that poem you writ t'other day,' says Joxer. 'Aw, it's a daarlin' poem, a daarlin' poem.'

And Boyle rises to his feet —

Shawn an' I were friends, sir, to me he was all in all,
His work was very heavy and the wages were very small.
None better on th' beach as Docker, I'll go bail,
'Tis now I'm feelin' lonely, for today he lies in jail.
He was not what some call pious — seldom at church or prayer;
For the greatest scoundrels I know, sir, goes every Sunday there.
Fond of his pint — well, rather, but hated the Boss by creed
But never refused a copper to comfort a pal in need.
MRS MADIGAN: Grand, grand; you should folley that up, you should folley that up.
BOYLE (*delightedly*): E-e-e-e-ch.

All this definition of character may be found in the printed text published here last Spring by Macmillan. Some of it exudes from the current performance at the Mayfair Theatre on a tiny stage that quite destroys the spaciousness of Mr O'Casey's drama. But those whose hopes had soared on the wings of enthusiastic reports from Dublin and London found the current production stale-mated — exacerbating to a degree. Not that the players did not discover the tentacles of meaning in the drama, nor that Mr Duncan as the strutting 'paycock' and Mr Cooper, especially, as the slippery 'Joxer' did not fill out the design of their parts. In these appreciative matters, virtually every actor in the cast revealed himself as beyond mere competency. But instead of a spirited performance to match the temper of the drama they played with little cohesion. In fact, the uncertainty of form in Mr O'Casey's technique was weakened, rather than strengthened, by the ineffectual direction. As a director, as well as an actor, Mr Duncan tends towards deliberation; he is inclined to reveal every corner of his part and performance rather than to weave the most homogeneous surfaces into a flowing pattern. In consequence, *Juno and the Paycock* alternately sagged and sputtered when it might have exhilarated by the sheer vigor of its undisciplined, creative force. The performance seemed merely the raw material from which an eclectic and refulgent acted version might be formed.

To introduce Mr O'Casey to Americans thus inauspiciously is more than commonly disheartening to those who entertain the most enthusiastic hopes for his future in the theatre. Far from being an intellectual, or handicapped by a dreary heap of academic tags and egregious theories, he comes fresh to the theatre from a youth of day-labor. His interest in the theatre was originally that of the amateur; nothing is more spontaneous and vigorous. In fact, the charm of *Juno* is chiefly a matter of spirit; the incidents, the twist of plot and the devices give out a strong odor of theatricalism. But the reflection of Mr O'Casey's own personality, his understanding and pity for his countrymen, his facility for perceiving the tragic affairs of the nation in terms of the average tenement household, betoken a brisk, refreshing dramatist of a people.

Ireland has already acclaimed him warmly, with encomiums and brickbats, according to its temperament; and the Abbey Theatre, for several years less forceful than usual, has given him a welcome typically Irish in its cordiality. Writing in *The Irish Statesman* of Mr O'Casey's new play, *The Plough and the Stars*, Walter Starkie summarizes the evolution of that influential theatre, with a racial pride no more obsequious than 'Captain' Boyle's:[2]

When gazing at the audience stacked in every corner of the Abbey Theatre last Monday night, it was impossible not to feel how direct is the influence exercised by the Abbey Theatre over Dublin life. And then we thought of three moments of the theatre in its evolution. At first it was poetry when poets dreamt in their ivory towers of far off legends heard faintly down the centuries. Then appeared *Countess Cathleen* and other plays. The stage had rediscovered poetry as its natural expression. Then descended the passionate temperament of Synge and made the Westernfolk speak in drama which gives the nourishment on which our imagination lives. Then followed the long list of playwrights who drew their inspiration from rustic scenes. Gradually the stage drama became more and more influenced by modern problems and became psychological in tendency. Now, in Sean O'Casey, there is the city drama as opposed to the traditional country drama, and it is no varnished tableau that he shows us, but the bitter, crude reality which he has observed in his walks through the streets. But Sean O'Casey is not a social dramatist like most of the moderns, filled with a desire to expose some vice and correct by developing one thesis in his play. He looks at our society from all sides and his fund of sympathy is large enough to include all. But though he pardons all, he never fails to expose hypocrisies and evil to the gaze of humanity. No dramatist is more characteristic if we want to show the difference between the English and the Irish artist.

NOTES

1. See pp. 27–9, Atkinson's article, 'Irish Folk in a Tragedy' (16 Mar. 1926).
2. Walter Starkie, '*The Plough and the Stars*', *Irish Statesman* (Dublin), V 23 (13 Feb. 1926) pp. 716–17.

Disillusion in Irish Drama*

Just before Sean O'Casey's *Juno and the Paycock* was mounted at the Mayfair Theatre in March,[1] his newest play, *The Plough and the Stars*, had a stormy premiere at the Abbey Theatre in Dublin.[2] Macmillans have recently published it in book form.[3] Its four acts reveal Mr O'Casey again inveighing against the futility of war, through the medium of the slum life most immediately affected by bloodshed. If he travels again the road so brutally laid down by *Juno and the Paycock* and confines himself to the same national problems and the same sort of characters, he writes even more grimly in the new play, with more passion and determina-

* *The New York Times* (16 May 1926).

tion. In *Juno* the silent hand of national warfare casts no really
ominous shadow until the last act; most of the play makes sym-
pathetic sport of the childish Boyle ménage, with a good deal of
bibulous merriment in the second act. The tragedy comes like a
knife thrust because, as far as the structure of the play is concerned, it is not retributive but gratuitous. In *The Plough and the
Stars*, however, Mr O'Casey begins to rattle the musket in the first
act, and rattles ever more vigorously in the succeeding three acts.
All the disillusion indicated in *Juno* pours like an angry flood
though the pages of the newly published volume.

Since Mr O'Casey keeps his own counsel and maintains no
hired claque of scribblers to sing his praises publicly, the sources
of information on this side of the Atlantic do not abound in
intimate chronicles of his life. He has been variously reported
here as a carpenter, janitor, electrician and plumber (such is the
romance of daily journalism) and his age has varied from 25 to
40. Until he became a playwright, more or less by chance, he
worked at whatever labor offered, and three times received the
'unemployment dole,' and he is now 40.[4] Some of the mystery
regarding the details of himself and his career began to life when
he went to London for the first time in his life several weeks ago,
to witness the London production of *The Plough*.[5] At that time
he was seen in the flesh by journalists who are not above telling
what they know. More specifically he visited by invitation the
venerable T.P.O'Connor, who wrote of him as 'The Prophet of
Disillusion' in T.P.'s and Cassell's Weekly. 'He is a striking figure
physically,' writes T.P., 'tall, thin, with a striking face — the eyes
very deep-set and very pensive, and the general expression rather
sombre.' More pertinent to the understanding of his plays is
T.P.'s later observation:

> Though he has conquered his difficulties, I should say that the
> iron has entered his soul; poverty has that effect on most men,
> and especially that form of poverty that means occasional
> hunger. This is the background of a sombre past in the slums of
> Dublin and in the ranks of workingmen — with whom employ-
> ment must necessarily be precarious — which gives to Mr
> O'Casey the pervasive spirit in all his plays. But there is a
> further factor which does not work in his mind alone, namely,
> the post-war spirit that reigns in Ireland as, though in a
> different form, it reigns with us.

Although one can only conjecture about the the effectiveness of *The Plough and the Stars* in the theatre, certainly the printed text promises a trenchant, piercing performance rendered ghastly by the 'red laugh.' For if Mr O'Casey has cut under the skin of his characters he has likewise painted internal warfare in blood-red tones that leave scant opportunity for chauvinistic defense. All the bloodshed and annihilation of families chronicled in the drama result from the malicious excitation of Dubliners by the voice of a man off-stage in the second act, a man speaking in magniloquent images of bogus results. 'Comrade soldiers of the Irish Volunteers and of the Citizen Army,' he says, 'we rejoice in this terrible war. The old heart of the earth needed to be warmed with the red wine of the battlefields.' Again: 'The last sixteen months have been the most glorious in the history of Europe. Heroism has come back to the earth. War is a terrible thing, but war is not an evil thing. People in Ireland dread war because they do not know it. Ireland has not known the exhilaration of war for over a hundred years. When war comes to Ireland she must welcome it as she would welcome the Angel of God!' Stirred up by this inflammatory drivel, the excitable volunteers and citizenry sweep off into the night crying, 'Death for the Independence of Ireland!' Off-stage during the remaining two acts the machine guns rattle, the wounded cry for the ambulance and fire crackles across the city. Without being subtle in his methods, Mr O'Casey gives the play the immediacy of his locale and the time of which he writes.

As in *Juno*, however, he points his moral in terms of the rabble, the 'slum lice,' one snob terms them, who are at once the means and the victims of the leaders. In the case of Commander Clitheroe and his 'little, little, red-lipped Nora,' Mr O'Casey reduces his dramatic conflict to personal and national loyalties by showing that devotion to the State is now synonymous with devotion to the home. In the idealistic community, of course, citizens fight for country to protect their homes. Mr O'Casey's weighing of forces makes rather for the opposite situation. Like Ibsen's modern-spirited heroine, this Nora seeks to draw the mask of passion across her husband's eyes when the summons comes from his military headquarters. 'No, no!' she exclaims, 'please, Jack; don't open it please, for your own little Nora's sake!' And later in the play, after fighting has broken out on all sides, Mr O'Casey uses this same passionate character to expose the futility of the military conflict and to report the spurious heroism of the volunteers. 'I tell you they're afraid to say they're afraid!' she says. 'Oh, I saw it. I saw it, Mrs Gogan. At the barricade in North Street I saw fear glowin' in all their eyes. An' in th' middle o' th' street was somethin' huddled up in a horrible tangled heap. His face was jammed again the stones, an' his arm was twisted around his back. An' every twist of his body was a cry against th' terrible thing that had happened to him. Ah' I saw they were afraid to look at it. An' some o' them laughed at me, but the laugh was a frightened one. An' some o' them shouted at me, but th' shout had in it th' shiver o' fear. I tell you they were afraid, afraid, afraid.' To fight without conviction, as the description indicates, it to play the fool, indeed. Written from this merciless point of view, no wonder *The Plough and the Stars* set up a furor at its first and second performances.

In *Juno and the Paycock*, it will be remembered, Boyle and Joxer return foolishly drunk, incapable of understanding, after the family fortunes have completely collapsed, and thus the tragedy stabs the innocent rather than the guilty. Similarly in *The Plough and the Stars* the most useless men-folk drink and play cards while their betters are dying in the streets outside. While the wounded are crying for mercy, the riff-raff of the tenements sing maudlin ballads and quarrel over their cards. Mr O'Casey uses every means at his disposal to underscore the stupidity of the local rebellion. None of the useless characters succumbs to the bullets; while Commander Clitheroe dies, and Bessie falls by a stray shot from the street, and Nora goes mad from a still-born child, the loafers play on and sing indifferently. Even the nobility of Commandant Clitheroe's death sounds empty by comparison with the misery he has already left in his home. 'He took it like a man,' the messenger reports impressively. 'His last whisper was to "Tell Nora to be brave; and that I'm ready to meet my God, an' that I'm proud to die for Ireland." An' when our General heard it he said that "Commandant Clitheroe's end was a gleam of glory." Mrs Clitheroe's grief will be a joy when she realizes that she has had a hero for a husband!' For the last twist of his dagger Mr O'Casey introduces two British Tommies, sullen and callous because they are strangers to the emotional family relationships already warmly portrayed before the audience. As the curtain falls they sip tea and sing 'Keep the Home Fires Burning,' quite unconscious of its irony.

Without seeing *The Plough and the Stars* in performance, one can be less sure of its artistic qualities than of its meaning. Probably Mr O'Casey has laid on his horrors too thick. Not the art of selection, but the zeal for completeness has led him into sweeping up every mordant detail; and no doubt his thoroughness robs his drama of the force of its message. For all his prophet-like significance, Mr O'Casey still lacks practice as a dramatist; and the force of his attack betokens a want of sensitiveness in play construction. His audiences on both sides of the Atlantic can put up with artistic clumsiness. His earnestness and rude strength are more useful in the theatre.

NOTES

1. See pp. 27–9, Atkinson's article, 'Irish Folk Life in a Tragedy (16 Mar. 1926).
2. World premiere, 8 February 1926, Abbey Theatre. Riots broke out on the third and fourth nights of the play.
3. Published 6 April 1926.
4. O'Casey, born in 1880, was forty-six years old at the time of this article.
5. English premiere, 12 May 1926, Fortune Theatre, London. O'Casey went to London to see a production of his play, *Juno and the Paycock*, which was transferred from the Royalty Theatre to the Fortune Theatre, 8 March 1926.

The Play*
O'CASEY AND THE IRISH PLAYERS

After two acts of pointless maundering around in music-hall humors, Sean O'Casey's *The Plough and the Stars*, put on at the Hudson last evening,[1] bites deep into the human tragedy of the Irish revolution. Acted by the Irish Players (with only an occasional hiss from the respectable gallery), Mr O'Casey's ragged drama, loosely contrived, leaves an uncertain impression until the evening is half done. When the preliminary fooleries are over, however, *The Plough and the Stars* speaks the bitter truth about

* *The New York Times* (29 Nov. 1927).

political bloodshed and human nature. Mr O'Casey, ex-brick-layer, ex-longshoreman, ex-laborer in general, writes with the rude strength of a hard-muscled workman. In respect to form *The Plough and the Stars* leaves a good deal to be desired. Its characterizations and its motives ring true.

Roughly speaking, his play, which now serves to introduce the Irish Players to America again, epitomizes the futility of revolution in the characters of Jack Clitheroe of the Irish Citizen Army and his wife. Whipped along by a vague chauvinistic emotionalism, Clitheroe resists the pleadings of his wife and leads his volunteer contingent in the street fighting of Easter Week, 1916, in Dublin. He is killed. His wife goes mad after losing her unborn child. At the final curtain, those who have suffered most are those who cared the least about the revolutionary principles.

But Mr O'Casey is no drawing-room playwright. His interests are national rather than personal and he turns *The Plough and the Stars* into an amorphous cartoon of Dublin tenement life. Painting in broad, bold brushfuls, he lays character on thick in the tenement house, in a public house, on the street and back in the house again. While the drama of Irish revolution cools its heels outside, Mr O'Casey makes merry with his carpenters, bricklayers, fruit vendors and charwomen, quarreling, guzzling liquor, flying at each other in temperamental rages, gabbling in big words over deep economic problems, tossing insults back and forth over religion, morals and politics.

Obviously Mr O'Casey lets his play get out of hand amid the squalid bravura of this racial comedy. *The Plough and the Stars* needs compression and unity. But there is no resisting the sturdy honesty of its characterization and the natural poetry of the dialogue. Even in her cups Bessie Burgess speaks in eloquent measures as she blasphemes the character of a sanctimonious charwoman. And Fluther Good, the excitable, bibulous carpenter, whose rattling tongue speaks endless nonsense, never once utters an unmusical sound. 'Talking like a book with its leaves torn out,' someone complains of him. They are all the same. And the playgoer, eager to be on with the story, grows impatient as the bickering scenes swirl on. But there is beauty in such dialogue, quite apart from its intelligence — the beauty of the chants and supplication. Mr O'Casey approaches his characters from the inside.

After hearing the lines spoken by the Irish Players, one cannot dissociate this drama from these actors. They are as natural in their flow of expression as the eloquence of the dialogue. Indeed, in one sense, *The Plough and the Stars* is less drama than sheer temperamental expression. As Fluther Good, the jabbering carpenter, Arthur Sinclair leads the company with his battered-derby characterization and his spurts of torrid conversation. But Sara Allgood as the broad-beamed fruit vendor and Maire O'Neill as the pious charwoman make quite as much of their hot-tempered parts, and Kathleen Drago as the conventional scarlet woman does not lag far behind. In several rather more cultivated parts, Shelah Richards, Sydney Morgan and Michael Scott lose none of the dynamic charm of Irish acting.

Mr O'Casey's play needs the discipline of art. One cannot blink the fact that its diffusion, and the long waits between scenes, frequently make for tedium in the first two acts. But the sincerity and the brutal, forceful tragedy of the last two acts carry a full load of meaning. Although Mr O'Casey does not preach he does not garble his message.

NOTES

1. Produced by the Irish Players for George C. Tyler at the Hudson Theatre, 28 November 1927. Total performances: 32

   Cast:

Fluther Good	Arthur Sinclair
Peter Flynn	J.A. O'Rourke
Mrs Gogan	Maire O'Neill
The Covey	Sydney Morgan
Nora Clitheroe	Shelah Richards
Bessie Burgess	Sara Allgood
Jack Clitheroe	Michael Scott
Capt. Brennan	Harry Hutchinson
Mollser	Margaret O'Farrell
A Bartender	E.J. Kennedy
Rosie Redmond	Cathleen Drago
The Figure in the Window	Joseph French
Lieut. Langon	Tony Quinn
Corporal Stoddart	Edwin Ellis
Sergeant Tinney	Joseph French

   Staged by Arthur Sinclair

The Play*

SEAN O'CASEY'S *THE PLOUGH AND THE STARS* PERFORMED BY THE IRISH PLAYERS

To appreciate the lumbering strength of *The Plough and the Stars*, which the Irish Players began to perform here last Monday,[1] we have only to recall Sean O'Casey's rigorous experience in life. As nearly everyone must know by this time, O'Casey became the most trenchant playwright of contemporary Ireland after a bitter apprenticeship in the ranks of labor. 'Though he has conquered his difficulties,' T.P.O'Connor said of him after an interview two years ago, 'I should say that the iron has entered his soul: poverty has that effect on most men, and especially that form of poverty that means occasional hunger. This is the background of a sombre past in the slums of Dublin and in the ranks of the workingman.' Before *Juno and the Paycock*, performed at the Abbey Theatre, transformed Mr O'Casey into one of the leading figures in the contemporary drama, he had sweated as a longshoreman, as a bricklayer, as a plumber, and he had sttod wearisomely in line for the unemployment dole. Naturally, there is 'muscular movement' in his play.

He does not accept his new station in life altogether in good part. Far from being ashamed of his past, he has the good sense to keep on living in its spirit. When he visited London for the first time, to see *Juno and the Paycock* played there, his contempt for formal evening dress alarmed Lady Londonderry's punctilious butler, who proposed to turn away the roughly attired guest of the evening. 'I think a dinner jacket and a hard shirt are among the funniest things in the world,' O'Casey confided to a big-eared reporter. 'I dined the other evening with Lady Lavery, Augustus John, the artist, and George Bernard Shaw and we did not wear evening dress. In fact, I think Mr Shaw wore kilts. But I will satisfy my insistent friends one day. I will wear evening dress in my coffin, as monks elect to wear their cowls when they die and go for their long repose.' When Mr O'Casey fearlessly approached the nuptial altar last September — no doubt as grim as ever — he abandoned his customary cap for a grey felt hat, but he retained

* The New York Times (4 Dec. 1927).

his sweater. Probably his bride promised to obey and probably she will.[2]

As acted by the Irish Players, *The Plough and the Stars* turns out to be exactly the sort of play Mr O'Casey's personality suggests — a robust, artless, pungent drama of Dublin tenement life. If it can be said properly to have a theme at all, it exposes the human costs of political revolution. In the last act one half-hearted revolutionist, who has confessed his weariness with the cause, dies from a shot through the lungs, his wife goes mad after a miscarriage, and the one innocent bystander who was always screaming her allegiance to the King is killed by a shot in the back. ''Ere, what' this, what's this?' exclaims the Tommy when he comes in and sees the body on the floor. 'Ow, Gawd, we've plugged one of the women of the 'ouse, Corporal Stoddard.' 'Whoy the 'ell did she gow to the window! Is she dead?' 'Ow, dead as bedammed. Well, we couldn't afford to toike any chawnce,' the Sergeant concludes phlegmatically. Everything about the revolution, on one side as well as the other, is as hopeless as that. Mr O'Casey does not spare the gall.

His finest achievement, however, is the creation of characters. No doubt Mr O'Casey is satirizing them a little as they double up their fists over a question of politics or pull hair over doubtful matters of personal honor. But Mr O'Casey's virtue as a dramatist is his strength not his subtlety, and his characters emerge as a particularly lively and amusing handful of Dubliners — hot-tempered, childish and upon necessity generous to the point of recklessness. How touchy they are on matters of religion! When the sophist of the crowd parades his meretricious learning about evolution, Fluther Good, the thick-headed carpenter, bursts into rage: 'You'll be kickin' an' yellin' for th' priest yet, me boyo. I'm not goin' to stand silent an' simple listenin' to a thick like you makin' a maddenin' mockery o' God Almighty. It 'ud be a nice derogatory thing on me conscience, an' me dyin', to look back in rememberin' of talkin' to a word-weavin' little ignorant yahoo of a red flag socialist!'

For all that an ecclesiastical and a poetical strain slips into the pothouse talk of even the most ignorant of the characters. Listen to the rhythms of Bessie Burgess's impersonal drunken slander upon Mrs Gogan's character. Low as its motives are, it is now a little King Jamesian in its phrasing: 'To look at some o' th' women that's knockin' about now is a thing to make a body sigh . . . A woman on her own, dhrinkin' with a bevy o' men is hardly an example to her sex... A woman dhrinkin' with a woman is one thing, an' a woman dhrinkin' with herself is still a woman — flappers may be put in another category altoghether — but a middle-aged woman makin' herself th' centre of a circle of men is a woman that is loud and stubborn, whose feet abideth not in her own house.'

In their second visit to America — their first was sixteen years ago — the Irish players bring actors rich in the quality of sweeping expression. No reading of *The Plough and the Stars* can yield the comedy and the fervor of the acted drama. As the ridiculous carpenter, whose one literary word is 'derogatory' for use in any connection, Arthur Sinclair fills out the lines until they fairly burst with comic intensity; and Maire O'Neill and Sara Allgood play their parts to the last drop of vitality. In such matters as lighting, stage setting and stage direction, this first performance of the Irish Players lacks skill. As a drama *The Plough and the Stars* lacks skill also. But if art is expression (and it is that among many other things) O'Casey's play and the Irish performance have a turbulent fluidity all their own.

NOTES
1. For production details, see pp. 38–40, Atkinson's article, 'The Play: O'Casey and the Irish Players' (29 Nov. 1927).
2. O'Casey and Eileen Reynolds Carey were married in the Roman Catholic Church of Our Most Holy Redeemer and St Thomas More, Cheyne Row, Chelsea, 23 September 1927.

The Play*
AGAIN THE IRISH PLAYERS

At the hands of the Irish Players, the second O'Casey play, *Juno and the Paycock*, put on with gusto at the Gallo Theatre last evening,[1] is rich in comedy, bitter in tragedy, poetic in dialogue,

* *The New York Times* (20 Dec. 1927).

pure gold in characters. Two years ago this first of the notable
O'Casey plays was mounted here by a ragbag troupe of actors who
tore it to tattered shreds.[2] Even now it is none too felicitous in its
sprawling appearance on a hugely cavernous stage and in a
theatre where the rumbling of the passing elevated trains from
time to time breaks the spell and drowns the cadenced music
from the stage.

What one can hear of it, however, rings as clear as a chime of
bells. As 'Captain' Jack Boyle, the shiftless garrulous butt of
O'Casey's satire and anger, Arthur Sinclair plays with rare high
spirit, with a command of racial comedy that is masterly. For no
matter how recklessly he lets himself go through the sweeping
flow of words set down for his part, he has it firmly under artistic
control as comedy no less than satire, as character portrayal just
on the intelligent side of burlesque. This is acting to be admired
in the measure it is enjoyed.

After witnessing the previous O'Casey play, *The Plough and
the Stars*, which comes next in the order of composition, no one
could mistake the authorship of *Juno and the Paycock*. Characterization, dialogue, point of view and style are the same. If the
theme is less searching in its indictment, the form is less rambling
by reason of its concern with the domestic tribulations of one
family. Once in the last act the national politics of Ireland reach
into the tenement home of the Boyle family and spirit Johnny
Boyle away to his doom. After two acts and a half of rollicking
comedy within doors, this swift fatal intrusion from the outside
comes like a smashing blow in the face. Mr O'Casey hits hard
when the right moment comes. There is no underestimating the
fierce strength of his attack.

Briefly, *Juno and the Paycock* romps through the comic fortunes of the Boyle family who inflate their standard of living on
the flimsy promise of a legacy and crash completely in the last act
when the legacy turns out to be an illusion. The time is 1922 and
the milieu is Dublin during the hostilities of the Free Staters and
the Republican Die-hards. By keeping national politics largely in
the background until the bitter, seemingly gratuitous conclusion,
Mr O'Casey makes them the more fiendish in their human
costliness.

His dramatic ideas are impulsively commonplace. We are
familiar with the promised legacy, and with the ambitious daughter of the tenements who is betrayed by a honey-lipped sophist

tricked out with cane and fine manners. Mr O'Casey's forte is characterization and dialogue by one who knows from personal experience the interior of a Dublin tenement.

Domestic brawls, neighborhood jollifications, impromptu singing, winged words on prosy subjects, ignorantly comic disquisitions on weighty themes beyond the knowledge of common men, malapropisms, the alluring majesty of death, rude curiosity, gossip and hot altercations spin through this episodic drama. 'Captain' Boyle, who can do more work with a knife and fork than with a shovel, who suffers from shooting pains in the legs when a job is in the offing; 'Joxer,' his ragged, snivelling, sycophantic retainer; Juno, his long-suffering but sharp-tongued wife; Mrs Maisie Madigan, the tippling upstairs neighbor — these are the joys of Mr O'Casey's play.

In spite of bad lighting and of direction that crowds all the action in one corner of the stage, the acting brings the play to vivid life. Sara Allgood as the wife and Maire O'Neill as the upstairs neighbor range from ingratiating and coy to vindictiveness. As Joxer, Sydney Morgan is delightfully slippery, backslapping and backstabbing, according to the prevailing winds. As Mary Boyle, the perilously ambitious daughter, Ria Mooney plays quietly and intelligently; and Harry Hutchinson, the apprehensive son, brings his part into proper proportion.

For American audiences, accustomed to rapidity in acting, the tempo of the Irish players seems vexatiously slow. Yet perhaps this results logically in the completeness of the character portrayal. Whatever the reason, the characters in *Juno and the Paycock* reveal a roundness and a fullness uncommon on our time-pressed stage.

NOTES

1. Produced by the Irish Players at the Gallo Theatre, 19 December 1927. Total performance: 40

Cast:	*'Captain' Jack Boyle*	Arthur Sinclair
	Juno Boyle	Sara Allgood
	Johnny Boyle	Harry Hutchinson
	Mary Boyle	Ria Mooney
	'Joxer' Daly	Sydney Morgan
	Mrs Maisie Madigan	Maire O'Neill
	'Needle' Nugent	J.A. O'Rourke
	Mrs Tancred	Cathleen Drago

Jerry Devine	Michael Scott
Charlie Bentham	E.J. Kennedy
An Irregular Mobilizer	Tony Quinn
Second Irregular Mobilizer	George Dillon
A Coal-block Vendor	Edwin Ellis
A Sewing Machine Man	Joseph French
Furniture Removal Men	William O'Connell
	Frank Donovan
Two Neighbors	Margaret O'Farrell
	Shelah Richards
Directed by	George C. Tyler

2. See pp. 30–4, Atkinson's column, 'O'Casey at the Bat: *Juno and the Paycock* — His First American Production' (21 Mar. 1926).

The Play*

O'CASEY'S WAR DRAMA

Somewhere amid the loose and flapping ends of *The Silver Tassie*, which was put on at the former Greenwich Village Theater last evening,[1] lie the materials of a stirring play. Most of Sean O'Casey's bitter comment on the war trickles away in his elliptical play construction, and the actors of The Irish Theatre, who are playing it, speak wretchedly. Much of the first act is lost in the speaking; all of the second act is verbally unintelligible, and only an occasional actor lifts the rich dialogue into the fluent beauty of Irish speech. On the whole, it is a sodden evening in Sheridan Square. But when O'Casey breaks through his own drama and the actors' performance, he emerges with that healthy, stalwart quality that is Elizabethan, fresh and strong; and you feel that muddled and disorderly as the play may be, it was composed in the fires of imagination. Especially in the last act, the brutal joining of tragedy to comedy, the natural exaltation of certain passages in the dialogue and the snatches of song persuade you that Mr O'Casey is no idle threat. He is a dramatist to be reckoned with.

* *The New York Times* (25 Oct. 1929).

The Silver Tassie is the work of that stormy Irishman whose *Juno and the Paycock* and *The Plough and the Stars* — broad and lusty comi-tragedies — once rejuvenated a dying Abbey Theatre and make a puissant dramatist of a laboring man. During the past two years it has been the subject of such a raging controversy that when you visit the theatre where it is playing you are likely to look more for stars than for drama. When the Abbey directorate refused it the furies broke loose. For O'Casey is not the man to weep tepid tears in a dark corner, and his head-thumping correspondence with Yeats[2] still keeps the smell of brimstone in the air. When *The Silver Tassie* was mounted two weeks ago in London,[3] with scenery by no less a Royal Academician than Augustus John,[4] the audience booed and frantic gentlemen clutched their headgear in self-protection. 'A hell of a play,' said Bernard Shaw, who is something in the roaring line himself. 'What I see is a deliberately phantasmopoetic first act, intensifying into a climax of war imagery in the second act, and then two acts of almost unbearable realism bringing down all the voodoo war poetry with an ironic crash to earth in ruins. There is certainly no falling off or loss of grip; the hitting gets harder and harder to the end.'

Let Mr Shaw speak for himself, as he is quite able to do. For most of us in Sheridan Square last evening, *The Silver Tassie* represents Mr O'Casey overreaching himself. In four acts he takes a handful of those turbulent Dubliners, of whom he has written with so much tang before, on to the battlefield, into the army hospitals and then home again to the cruel indifference of post-war revelry. For comedy there are the chicken-hearted braggarts who are still intoxicated with their burst of words. For tragedy there is young Harry Heegan, who won the silver cup three times for the Avondale Football Club in Dublin. He is paralyzed from the waist down in the war. When he comes home in a wheelchair he can only look on while his spirited sweetheart goes dancing off with another veteran, and shout his torment and strike out angrily against the heartlessness of his fate. For it is in the last act that Mr O'Casey gathers up all his scattered materials of fashions them into compact form.

If the performance were intelligible it might be possible to catch the significance of the second act when Mr O'Casey turns from realism into pure expressionism. While the guns are thundering in the background, the soldiers in the trenches chant, sing, mock in unison and speak in series the clipped sentences peculiar to this subjective style of writing. But in this act, particularly the miserable diction leaves you completely at sea, and what must be intended to symbolize the gratuitous futility to warfare slumps into complete verbal incoherence on the stage.

Even when Mr O'Casey is on the more familiar ground of realism his drama sprawls considerably, and brings no glib theme out of the disorder. That is what keeps people away from the theatre. But those who may be interested in Mr O'Casey's personality will find good evidence here of his indomitable strength, his passionate nature, his hatred of the sham of war — and his command of a racy, highly figured style of dialogue.

Several of the actors snared into the new Irish Theatre, which is now making its first production, are particularly good. As Harry Heegan, Sherling Oliver plays with the power that is O'Casey's. Margaret Barnstead gives a conspicuously good performance as a religious fanatic. Allyn Gillyn puts high color into the heedless youthfulness of the sweetheart. And if intelligibility were not the first requisite of acting, you might feel kindly toward the racial comedy of Sean Dillon and Eddie O'Connor.

The broad Dublin accent is not an easy one for New Yorkers to understand. But the Irish company that played *The Plough and the Stars* here two years ago made it understandable as well as beautiful. Before a local Irish theatre can attract a polyglot Manhattan audience, it must clarify its speech. And before you can make up your mind fully about *The Silver Tassie*, you must hear it in an accomplished performance.

NOTES

1. Produced by the Irish Theatre, Inc., at the Irish Theatre, 24 October 1929. Total performances: 51

Cast:		
Sylvester Heegan	Sean Dillon
Mrs Heegan	Emma Conrow
Simon Norton	Edward O'Connor
Susie Monican	Margaret Barnstead
Mrs Foran	Kitty Collins
Teddy Foran	Ralph Cullinan
Harry Heegan, D.C.M.	Sherling Oliver
Jessie Taite	Allyn Gillyn
Barney Bagnal	David Keating
Kevin Kearney	John Ferris

The Croucher	Schuyler MacGuffin
1st Soldier	James Metcalfe
2nd Soldier	John Ferris
3rd Soldier	Ned Lane
4th Soldier	Ralph Cullinan
The Corporal	Francis Kennelly
The Visitor	Abram Gillette
The Staff Wallah	L.H. Dennison
1st Stretcher-Bearer	Pendleton Harrison
2nd Stretcher-Bearer	Harry Wallace
3rd Stretcher-Bearer	John Wynne
4th Stretcher-Bearer	Dajalna Montana
1st Casualty	Patrick Glasgow
2nd Casualty	Leonard Austin
Surgeon Forby Maxwell	Bertram Millar
The Sister of the Ward	Ennis Clare

Staged by Miceal Breathnach

2. For the complete correspondence surrounding the rejection of the play, see *The Letters of Sean O'Casey*, vol. 1, David Krause (ed.) (London: Cassell; New York: Macmillan, 1975).

3. *The Silver Tassie* had its world premiere at the Apollo Theatre, London, 11 October 1929. Staged by C.B. Cochran, directed by Raymond Massey.

4. John did the scenery for the controversial second act. The other three acts were done by G.E. Galthorp.

Making or Breaking O'Casey*

No doubt, we should be duly grateful to the newly organized Irish Theatre for taking Sean O'Casey's *The Silver Tassie* out of book form and putting it on the stage of the former Greenwich Village Theatre where all who have eyes can look at it. After the phlegmatic public response to *Juno and the Paycock* and *The Plough and the Stars*, acted here two years ago by such racy mummers as Sara Allgood, Maire O'Neill and Arthur Sinclair, it is not likely that we shall ever see his plays except through the good offices of especially interested organizations. Although New York does not take kindly to naturalistic Irish playing, the Irish temperament is

* *The New York Times* (10 Nov. 1929).

closer kin to drama than any other in the Western world; it burns
with the divine dramatic fire. What Swift called 'the affectation
of politeness' does not curb its natural impulsiveness. But New
Yorkers do not want Irish drama in numbers sufficient to pay
boat fares and operating expenses.

In these circumstances we probably would be grateful to the
Irish Theatre if the performance mumbled incoherently into the
scenery in Sheridan Square conveyed much of the drama O'Casey
has written. With the exception of such able or magnetic actors as
Margaret Barnstead, Sherling Oliver and Allyn Gillyn, the
players conceal the dialogue in thick-tongued speaking of a
brogue that eludes the ears even of those who are familiar with it.
Nor has the direction mastered the surface clutter of the writing.
It has not failed completely: if you read the play after seeing the
performance you perceive that Miceal Breathnach has understood the contrast in moods and inflections in the realistic por-
tions of the text. But the second act, written in a form of symbolic
expressionism, has overwhelmed him and his actors. Excepting a
few moments when the gusty bravado of O'Casey's personality
comes to the surface, the performance of *The Silver Tassie* is only
a shade more articulate than the text published last year by
Macmillan.

The failure of the Sheridan Square performance is all the more
disappointing in view of the general respect with which *The Silver
Tassie* has been received recently in London.[1] Under the management of C.B. Cochran, Raymond Massey has directed a performance that forces the meaning out of O'Casey's furious play, and
in particular resolves the truncated recitatives of the second act
into what Charles Morgan describes as 'illusion clear of the
naturalistic plane.'[2] St John Ervine has discussed the play with
tolerant admiration in *The Observer*.[3] In *The Saturday Review*
Ivor Brown describes the much disputed second act as 'a gunpow-
der sonata, which shall be both a litany of the damned and an
outline of all human agony in silhouetted cartoon.' 'The play is in
some ways clumsy,' says Mr Brown, 'But so is a giant.'[4] Never was
there more concrete evidence that production can make or break
a play.

For O'Casey is above everything a theatrical dramatist. In 'the
delicate quietness of your own home,' to use Simon Norton's
comic phrase in the first act, O'Casey's thinking and dramatic
structure may not appeal to your sweet sense of reason. When the

Abbey Theatre directorate rejected *The Silver Tassie* in the Spring of 1928 after reading the typed manuscript, it was domestic reason operating against the defiant rodomontade of O'Casey's theatrical style. 'You have no subject,' Yeats wrote in a foolscap of objections to the play. Even Walter Starkie, dramatic critic of *The Irish Statesman*, who read the manuscript during that pate-punching Irish Spring, believed the characters to be unreal. But while Yeats and [Lennox] Robinson were regretting the falling off in power of the last two acts and voting against *The Silver Tassie* for production, Mr Starkie was counseling with a temperate wisdom that does great credit to his powers of discernment. 'It is written around a great and noble idea', he was saying under date of April 30, 1928.[5] And in spite of certain glaring faults 'I feel that the author is experimenting in a new world of drama. . . . Sean O'Casey has given us so many fine works that we ought to leave the final decision with the audience that has laughed and wept with him. He is groping after a new drama outside the conventional stage; at any moment he may make a great discovery.'

His point is so clairvoyant that it should be straightway canonized as a critical principle. When a dramatist has given such stirring proof of his powers as *Juno and the Paycock* he is entitled to whatever indiscretions in form and subject matter he chooses. Even if they weaken the force of his dramatic statement, as it seems to me they do in *The Silver Tassie*, they do not seriously question his ability, nor his right to experiment in new forms and materials. If they fail, the burden of proof is not upon him but upon his critics. Ultimately he is probably a better judge than they are. They know what they like, which is interesting. But if he is a man of integrity, like O'Casey, he will soon know what is right and what is wrong with his work, and that is all that matters in the development of a dramatic career.

As the London production of *The Silver Tassie* proves, O'Casey is no knocker-together of joint-pieces for dramatic entertainment; he has none of the 'sin and sachet' of the ten-cent poetaster. In any survey of the modern drama he is one of the figures to be reckoned with. It is not many years since he was exciting Dublin as the laboring man turned playwright whose *Juno and the Paycock* and *The Plough and the Stars* were revitalizing the Abbey Theatre — an audacious writer with the sweat and muscle of the workingman, a fulminator whose plays were dissolved in the bitters of the Irish Revolution. If those who mistake drama for mansuetude expected that O'Casey had shot his bolt with the Irish Revolution, they reckoned without the pugnacity and determination of his personality. He takes the drama more seriously than the academicians; he works at it — dressed in a gray sweater. He is steeped in Shakespeare and the other Elizabethans. 'I would make it a penal offense,' he exclaimed recently to a correspondent of *The Observer*, 'for any man to write a play without being able to declaim two or three of Shakespeare's plays by heart. . . . Shakespeare was my education.'[6] You might gather as much from the robustiousness of the rude poetry that thrusts its way into his dialogue.

In short, Mr O'Casey is the most exhilarating personality in the English-speaking drama today. Perhaps Mr Cochran and Arch Selwyn, his American associate, may be persuaded to bring over their London production of *The Silver Tassie* before this season is over. Whatever its reception, it would do them more honor than their recent futile importation of *The Middle Watch*.

NOTES

1. *The Silver Tassie* had its world premiere at the Apollo Theatre, London, 11 Oct. 1929.
2. Charles Morgan, 'Apollo Theatre: *The Silver Tassie*, A Tragi- Comedy by Sean O'Casey', *The Times* (London) 12 Oct. 1929, p. 8.
3. St John Ervine, 'Mr O'Casey's Passion Play. Apollo: *The Silver Tassie*', *Observer* (London), 13 Oct. 1929, p. 15.
4. Ivor Brown, '*The Silver Tassie* by Sean O'Casey: Apollo Theatre', *Saturday Review* (London), 19 Oct. 1929, pp. 446–7.
5. For the complete text of Starkie's letter see *The Letters of Sean O'Casey*, vol. I, David Krause (editor) (London: Cassell and New York: Macmillan, 1975), pp. 274–5.
6. '*The Silver Tassie*', *Observer* (6 Oct. 1929) p. 13.

The Play*

'TATTERDEMALIONS OF DUBLIN IN *JUNO AND THE PAYCOCK*'

To those of us who are retentive enough to remember the Irish Players in *Juno and the Paycock* five years ago, the performance staged last evening at the Martin Beck by the Abbey Theatre troupe[1] is, as Captain Jack would say, 'a bit of a disappointment.' Arthur Sinclair, Maire O'Neill, Sara Allgood and the late Sydney Morgan left the standards for O'Casey plays unreasonably high. Sufficient as the present company is, it lacks the gusty comedy of its predecessors, and it has less iron for the bitter tragedy at the end. If you cherish the memory of glorious occasions you miss the music of speech that turned *Juno and the Paycock* into a rowdy poem and the anguished cry of a stricken country when it was done here before. Although the horseplay in the current revival is funny enough to keep you rocking in your seat it is, alas, no match for the broadly-sustained exuberance that competed with the elevated railway clatter in what used to be the Gallo Theatre.

With that chilling observation the bill of exceptions is hereby finished. For *Juno and the Paycock* is a roaring drama, whoever plays it, and the tragedy in the third act is all the blacker because O'Casey does not bathe it in tears. Particularly in the opening act Barry Fitzgerald is uproariously funny, two steps across the borderline of farce. Never was there such a tatterdemalion figure, with pants that hang in loose wrinkles, a ragged coat, that has long since abandoned pretensions and a cap turned sideways on the head. Mr Fitzgerald has built the colossal fraud of his captain into a stiff, broad-shouldered figure whose ignorant pride stares out of one of the most querulous countenances ever made up.

This Abbey Theatre comedian puts nothing between him and a sound guffaw. He turns comedy into a spacious lampoon. And when you consider what a comic fellow the captain is you realize that he is fair game for lusty playing. For Captain Jack Boyle, who can do more work with a knife and a fork than with a shovel, has a pride of the most stupendous grandeur. He is the centre of his universe. In the last act he comes staggering in after a merry session at Foley's snug, and looking about at a reeling world he

* *The New York Times* (20 Oct. 1932).

says authoritatively: 'The world will have to settle itself.' And that is the touchstone to his character. He wriggles out of jobs, talks expansively of his heroism at sea, stands on the ceremony of the man of the world when he is in a tight position and philosophizes with deep satisfaction beside the few coals of his tenement fire. While his family sinks into misery and tragedy, the captain complacently observes: 'The world is in a state of chassis.' He is a grand figure, rich in unconscious humor, savagely ironic in his significance. Mr Fitzgerald plays him to the hilt.

To play him so broadly is a great temptation. After roaring with amusement during the first act this department is in no position to cavil. But Captain Jack does throw the rest of the performance out of perspective. Eileen Crowe is a rather pallid Juno, and F.J. McCormick has nothing more vivid than a shrug and a raffish slipperiness in the part of Joxer. Only a bulging, preening figure like Maureen Delany's Maisie Madigan can hold its own against so robust a Captain Jack. And when you come to the tragic cataclysm of the third act you have only the faintest notion of how brutal a writer O'Casey can be when he turns full in the face of Ireland. Unless comedy is held in sound restraint it can blight the soberer thoughts of an ironic indictment.

On the whole, the Abbey Theatre troupe has a spirit that is heartening to feel. Kate Curling has not only beauty enough to play the daughter but the ability to give a character all its facets, to keep it alive even when the play neglects it and to relate it harmoniously to the whole. . . .

NOTES

1. Revived by the Abbey Theatre Irish Players under the management of Alber & Wickes, Inc. at the Martin Beck Theatre. The Players were in New York from 17 October until 12 November 1932, and *Juno and the Paycock* alternated with Lennox Robinson's *The Whiteheaded Boy* and *The Far Off Hills*; Lady Gregory's *The Rising of the Moon*; J.M. Synge's *The Playboy of the Western World*; and Paul Vincent Carroll's *Things That Are Caesar's*. Atkinson reviewed the 19 October performance of *Juno*.

Cast:	
Captain Jack Boyle	Barry Fitzgerald
Juno Boyle	Eileen Crowe
John Boyle	Arthur Shields
Mary Boyle	Kate Curling
'Joxer' Daly	F.J. McCormick
Mrs Maisie Madigan	Maureen Delany

'Needles' Nugent	Una Wright
Mrs Tancred	May Craig
Jerry Devine	P.J. Carolan
Charlie Bentham	Michael J. Dolan
An irregular	Denis O'Dea

The Play*

'SEAN O'CASEY'S FIRST DRAMA ACTED FOR THE FIRST TIME IN NEW YORK'

Although *Juno and the Paycock, The Plough and the Stars,* and *The Silver Tassie* have been acted in New York, Sean O'Casey's first play, *Shadow of a Gunman*, has somewhat eluded 'the crossroads of the world' until the Abbey Theatre mounted it at the Martin Beck Theatre Saturday evening.[1] As a play it is less firmly rooted in character than its two illustrious successors, but obviously it is cut from the same pattern. Set in a slatternly Dublin tenement in 1920 it brings to the stage the same garrulous, shiftless people; the same gusty humor enlivens the dialogue and the same ironic tragedy smolders under the comedy at the end. Even without *Juno and the Paycock*, which enriches the figures and the colors of O'Casey's pattern, you would recognize *Shadow of a Gunman* as the work of a man of extraordinary stature. Now he is partially blind and he is living apart from his country-men in London; and it may be that his best work is already finished. But as long as there are Irish comedians like Arthur Sinclair, Barry Fitzgerald and F.J. McCormick *Juno and the Paycock* will be one of the great realistic plays of this century.

In the earlier play Donal Davoren is *Shadow of a Gunman*. Although he is really a poet, the other tatterdemalions in his tenement believe him to be a political revolutionary hiding away from the military authorities. Since that impression makes him the hero of the house and attracts Minnie Powell to him he does nothing to correct it. But it fills him with alarm when the British

* *The New York Times* (31 Oct. 1932).

soldiers raid the house that night. Looking around to make sure that the room contains nothing that might excite a soldier's suspicions, he discovers to his horror that the bag left under his roommate's bed that morning is filled with bombs. It is the property of his roommate's friend. To protect Davoren, Minnie Powell takes it into her room, where she thinks it will be safe from the raiders. But they find it, take Minnie away on their lorry, and she is shot in an ambush encountered along the road. The savage, rebuking irony of *Shadow of a Gunman* lies in the fact that the innocent are again the victims of political warfare; and the two men who are responsible for Minnie's arrest, and inadvertently responsible for her death, are too cowardly to stand up in her defense.

That is the plot. But you have to look sharp to distinguish it. For the humor is wild and continuous; it almost smothers the tragedy of the conclusion. And although Davoren is the shadow of the gunman, Seumas Shields, a prattling peddler, is the more conspicuous of the two chief characters in the play. At least, he is in Mr McCormick's lusty comic acting. Half way through the first act Shields rises with a groan from the ragged bed on which he is discovered at the rising of the curtain, dresses carelessly in the dirty tatters of the type, and eventually shuffles lazily out with his battered bag of peddler's supplies. But throughout the entire second act, which is the longer, he never gets out of bed. Yet the talk never subsides for an instant. And what talk it is! Boastful, belligerent, peevish, unctuous, dogmatic, philosophical — and comic withal. Although it sounds realistic, it is bursting with humor, and it has an ironic overtone. Chattering in bed, Mr McCormick gives it all the restless, impromptu inflections of human character. Pungent as the part is, he makes it inordinately funny with his twitching, his shrugs and sighs and his bland vocal tones.

As usual, the Abbey Theatre company plays with rare harmony and perfect recognition of character. Arthur Shields gives one of his most direct performances as the reputed gunman. Maureen Delany and Barry Fitzgerald give their tenement types the savor of humanity and uncommon comic breadth. Although *Shadow of a Gunman* is not O'Casey at his best, it is a racy sequence of comic writing, and night after night this Irish company reveals the green pliant beauty of life.

NOTES

1. Presented by the Abbey Theatre Irish Players under the management of
   Alber and Wickes, Inc. at the Martin Beck Theatre, 29 October 1932.
   Preceded by *Cathleen ni Houlihan*, by W.B. Yeats.

Cast:		
	Donal Davoren	Arthur Shields
	Seumas Shields	F.J. McCormick
	Tommy Owens	Michael J. Dolan
	Adolphus Grigson	P.J. Carolan
	Mrs Grigson	Maureen Delany
	Minnie Powell	Eileen Crowe
	Mr Mulligan	Una Wright
	Mr Maguire	Denis O'Dea
	Mrs Henderson	May Craig
	Mr Gollogher	Barry Fitzgerald
	An Auxillary	Denis O'Dea

Projector for a Fantasy*

O'CASEY'S *WITHIN THE GATES*, A DRAMATIC DANCE OF REPRESENTATIVE MEN AND WOMEN — THE QUALITY OF HIS MERCY

If the theatre is trivial, the reason is clear. The great themes are difficult to express. The journeyman playwright who is blessed with facility and flair can produce without much difficulty the bits of fluff that keep the theatres lighted. But when he is burning with some great poetic emotion about the destiny of mankind on this wretched little planet he discovers that the ordinary dramatic molds are inadequate, and he is under the necessity of creating something bold enough for his theme. This, it seems to me, has been the problem that Sean O'Casey has had to face in his newly published drama, *Within the Gates*, copies of which, published by Macmillan, have just arrived in this country. Mr O'Casey has striven to get closer to the sources of good and evil than he did in *Shadow of a Gunman, Juno and the Paycock* and *The Plough and the Stars*. He has gone one step further than he did in *The*

* *The New York Times* (31 Dec. 1933).

Silver Tassie by translating his emotions into a sort of symbolic
dance of representative characters with music and song. His
theme is the biggest one he has conjured with. His conception of
the theatre as an organ with many stops, capable of speaking in
many voices, makes *Within the Gates* the most virtuoso project
the theatre has had to face in some years. And yet it seems to me
that *Within the Gates* is not completely fulfilled. Although Mr
O'Casey's voice echoes through it passionately, and his hatred and
faith have the conviction of prophecy, he has not mastered his
theme. Mr O'Casey's style cannot cope with the flaming tumult
of his feeling.

   Although I have read the text carefully twice, I am not certain
that I understand all that Mr O'Casey is saying. The four sets of
Within the Gates are laid in a London park during the four seasons of the year. All its men and women are impersonal represen-
tatives of types of human character — The Dreamer, The
Bishop, The Atheist, The Young Whore, A Young Salvation
Army officer, etc. Against the background of Mr O'Casey's mystic
affirmation of life there is a conventional thread of story, center-
ing around the miseries and the aspirations of The Young Whore.
She is the illegitimate daughter of The Bishop and the step-
daughter of The Atheist, and she wants to marry The Gardener,
who has no intention of settling down. In a world dominated by
church and State, which impose fixed rules of conduct on in-
dividuals she swears that she will be the mistress of her soul and
meet death with dancing. Only The Dreamer, who is a poet, can
minister to the needs of her spirit. The church will not help here
unless she confesses herself beaten. All the established authorities
of church and State try to push her into the ghastly company of
The Down-and-Outs, whose macabre chant pursues the various
episodes of Mr O'Casey's play. But when death finally comes for
her The Dreamer helps her to meet it with dancing. As soon as
she is dead the church gives her its blessing.

   This is only the sketchiest outline of *Within the Gates*, which is
really a human pageant. Since the substance of the play is
reported literally in the preceding paragraph, it is no fair
indication of Mr O'Casey's purposes. For, among other things, he
seems to be declaring his faith in the courage and spirit of nature
and man and his hatred for established institutions. While
England goes to her doom the church and the State cling fatu-
ously to conventional rules of conduct and the thinkers quibble

over the meshing of ideas that are beyond them. Here men and women scurry without direction according to their myriad impulses. With the passion of an Old Testament prophet, Mr O'Casey pronounces a death sentence upon this materialist age. The Old Woman replies to one of the park orators in these baleful words:

> There can be nor rest nor work nor play where there is no life; and the golden infancy of England's life is tarnishing now in the bellies of the worms. ... Your politics are husks that only swine will eat; your power's behind a battlement of hunger; your religion's as holy as a colored garter round a whore's thigh; truth's bent in two and hope is broken. O Jesu, is there no wisdom to be found anywhere! All gone with the golden life of England into the bellies of the worms!

And behind the dance of the play there is always the chant of The Down-and-Outs sounding like the funeral march of the old civilization:

> We challenge life no more with our dead faiths or our dead hope; We carry furled the flags of our dead hope and our dead faith; Day sings no song, neither is there room for rest, beside night in her sleeping;
> Life has left us but a sigh for a song, and a deep sigh for a drum-beat!

In short, Mr O'Casey has written the sort of dramatic adumbration that most of us would delight in heralding as a masterpiece. Instead of frittering around with the easy types of dramatic craftsmanship he has resolutely come to grips with an extremely difficult form of shapes and echoes and rhythms. And instead of temporizing with modern thought he has turned angrily against casuistry and cant. There is something remarkably exhilarating about the force of the mind behind the fantasy. It has a Shakespearean relish of the comedy and tragedy of mankind. Once Mr O'Casey was a day laborer in Dublin. There is still the iron strength of a workingman in his writing. His emotions are vehement. He has the high moral fervor of a man who is a churchman at heart, whatever his thinking may be. In a world that is noisy with petty disputes over methods of procedure Mr O'Casey's capacity for capturing the whole scene in terms of representative men is chastening and illuminating. Masterly stage direction might fuse all the scrabbled details of the drama into a noble design of living people.

But there are problems. Mr O'Casey has not mastered his material. He is susceptible to appearances. He is unable to penetrate to the inner life of all his characters. He clutters his last act with burlesque arguments. He seems to me unable at times to distinguish between what is vital to his theme and what is trivial. His passion does not burn with a clear flame. That is why I believe that *Within the Gates* is not fulfilled, although in view of Mr O'Casey's audacious project, what he has done may be enough.

The Play*

FANTASY OF THE SEASONS IN HYDE PARK IN SEAN O'CASEY'S *WITHIN THE GATES*

Let us face this thing boldly. Sean O'Casey has written a great play in *Within the Gates*, which was staged at the National last evening.[1] Being contemptuous of the petty depravities of the popular theatre, he has written a fantasy of Hyde Park, where he has imprisoned the full savor of life. When the text of *Within the Gates* was published last year,[2] it seemed to many of us that Mr O'Casey, who once wrote such biting plays as *Juno and the Paycock* and *The Plough and the Stars*, had overreached himself in a poetic medium beyond his strength. But out of the dead print of the text a glorious drama rose last evening with songs and dances, with colors and lights, with magnificent lines that cried out for noble speaking. For Mr O'Casey is right. He knows that the popular theatre has withered, and he also has the gift to redeem it with a drama that sweeps along through the loves and terrors of mankind. *Within the Gates* is a testament of Mr O'Casey's abiding faith in life. Nothing so grand has risen in our

* *The New York Times* (23 Oct. 1934).

impoverished theatre since this reporter first began writing of plays.

To people accustomed to the racy statements of the realistic drama it will be difficult to describe Mr O'Casey's fantasy. It is set in Hyde Park and divided into four parts representing the seasons. There, amid the trees, flowers and benches, and in the shadow of the grim statue of a soldier, Mr O'Casey discovers the people who represent the whole gamut of life — a poet, a Bishop, an atheist, a Salvation Army officer, unemployed, soap-box orators, nursemaids, soldiers, the tortured, ghastly train of the down-and-outs whose ominous, drum-beat melody is forever stealing through the park and striking terror in the hearts of the people loitering there.

If Mr O'Casey has any specific story, it concerns the poet, the Bishop and the whore. Being sick in body and broken in heart, she is desperately in need of assistance. The Bishop can give her nothing but sanctimonious counsel. But the poet can give her understanding and share with her the few comforts that are his; and when the demoniac down-and-outs reach out for her the poet can drive them back by the force of his spiritual serenity. If there is a story in *Within the Gates*, that is it.

But Mr O'Casey is in search of many other things. Being a man of natural courage, he has opened the heart of *Within the Gates* to all the men who walk the earth and he has written fluid verses in which they can sing their affirmations and he has carved prose out of gold, Shakespeare and the Bible. Sitting in the park, he is aware of everything and he relishes it, for, among modern dramatists, he is the man who is completely alive. There is the low comedy of the street-corner philosophers. There is the timid middle-class propriety of the nursemaids. There is the selfish lust of the gardener and the slippery corruption of the young man in plus-fours. There is the venomous contempt and bitterness of the unemployed. Above all this, like the steam of the spring, hovers Mr O'Casey's faith in the endurance of life. For God is his greatest character. By implication Mr O'Casey has set all the fragments of Hyde Park life in universal perspective.

Dialogue is only a scratch on the surface of a play of this heroic stature. Being the theatre of spiritual magnificence, it needs all the glories of stage art, and it has them in this superb production. Last year *Within the Gates* was drably produced in London.[3] Here George Bushar and John Tuerk, who deserve to be knighted, have given it a memorable production, directed with rare sensibility by Melvyn Douglas. The incidental music by Milton Lusk and A. Lehman Engel enkindles the drama as much as anything Mr O'Casey has written. The songs have a purity of meaning; the chant for the down-and-outs is macabre. As the designer of the settings and costumes, James Reynolds has understood the problem of fantasy in all its ramifications, and endowed *Within the Gates* with a decor that lifts it into visual eminence. Elsa Findlay's dance arrangements are pitiably inadequate; they are twittering preciosities that should be flung out of the production instantly.

Fortunate in most of his collaborators, Mr O'Casey is likewise fortunate in his actors, who have been splendidly directed. As the tortured young woman, Lillian Gish gives a performance instinct with the spirit of the drama. Never did an actress play a part with more sincerity or deeper comprehension. As the poet, whom Mr O'Casey describes as the dreamer, Bramwell Fletcher brilliantly avoids the maudlin quagmires of the part. Moffat Johnston's bishop is a strong, clear, illuminating performance. As a slatternly old woman, Mary Morris plays superbly with a hint of the grand manner in tragedy. Ralph Cullinan has a voice that is perfect in tone for a play of this sort; as the foreman of the garden, he can impregnate a speech with the virtue of fantasy. John Daly Murphy gives a pungent performance as a park derelict. Phil Bishop introduces a hearty note of comedy as a querulous park sage. Byron McGrath's Salvation Army officer is soberly persuasive. In the long cast it would be hard to find a single actor who does not measure up to his part of the theme.

But all this merely reinterates the fundamental fact that Mr O'Casey has written a great play. There is iron in its bones and blood in its veins and lustre in its flesh, and its feet rest on the good brown earth. In fact, it is a humbling job to write about a dynamic drama like *Within the Gates*.

NOTES

1. Produced by George Bushar and John Tuerk at the National Theatre, 22 October 1934.

Cast:	The Dreamer	Bramwell Fletcher
	The Bishop	Moffat Johnston
	The Bishop's Sister	Kathryn Collier
	1st Chair Attendant	Barry Macollum

2nd Chair Attendant	John Daly Murphy
A Boy	Alexander Lewis
The Atheist	Morris Ankrum
The Policewoman	Jessamine Newcombe
The Young Man in Plus-Fours	Ralph Sumpter
The Scarlet Woman	Miriam Goldina
1st Nursemaid	Vera Fuller Mellish
2nd Nursemaid	Esther Mitchell
A Guardsman	James Jolley
The Gardner	Barry Kelley
1st Evangelist	Edward Broadley
2nd Evangelist	Arthur Villars
The Young Whore	Lillian Gish
A Young Salvation Army Officer	Byron McGrath
The Foreman	Ralph Cullinan
The Old Woman	Mary Morris
The Man in the Bowler Hat	Stanley G. Wood
The Man with the Stick	Phil Bishop
The Man in the Trilby Hat	Charles Angelo
1st Platform Speaker	Gordon Gould
2nd Platform Speaker	Dodson Mitchell
A Young Man	Arthur Gould Porter
The Man in the Burberry	Charles Keane

A Chorus of Down-and-Outs, Young Men and Girls, Salvationists, Strollers in the Park, etc.

> Mildred Albert, Suzanne Black, Mary Brandt, Kathryn Curl, Martha Eaton, Betty Gladstone, Anne Goddard, Dorothy Higgins, Marjorie Hyder, Ellen Love, Elizabeth Morgan, Evangeline Raleigh, Ursula Seiler, Edith Shayne, Virginia Spottswood, Pauline Stokes, Peggy Strickland, Teddy Williams, George Augustin, Tony Barone, Mordecae Bauman, Victor Bryant, Tomes Chapman, Frank Gabrielson, Kenneth Bostock, Serge Gradoff, Serge Inga, Robert Kerr, Stanley Klein, Karl Kohrs, Ram Meyer, Gifford Nash, William Trieste, Clyde Walters, William Williams, Rodifer Wilson.

Symbol of the Seasons	Margaret Mower
The Woman Who Feeds the Birds	Ellen Larned

Staged by Melvyn Douglas
Setting by James Reynolds
Dance direction by Elsa Findlay
Incidental music by Milton Lusk and A. Lehman Engel

2. See pp. 57–60, Atkinson's article, 'Projector for a Fantasy' (31 Dec. 1933).

3. World premiere, Royalty Theatre, London, 7 February 1934. Directed by Norman MacDermott.

*Within the Gates**

SEAN O'CASEY'S FANTASY OF HYDE PARK — DRAMA OF LIFE AS THEY LEAD IT OUT-OF-DOORS

Inscrutable are the ways of Providence. For years the gentry idling in the studios have dreamed dispassionately of a brave, many-voiced form of drama that would plunge deeper and soar higher than nervous realism and employ singing and dancing as handmaids of the stage. The man who has at last worked the miracle received his early training, not in the classrooms or ateliers, but on the streets and docks and in the tenements of Dublin. Sean O'Casey's *Within the Gates*, which is now on view at the National Theatre,[1] has given the drama greater compass and a more exalted spirit than any new drama I have seen. Since there is keen difference of opinion about Mr O'Casey's fantasy, this chronicle may as well be presented as an expression of personal opinion. And the fact is that in my experience as a professional playgoer the plays I remember with the deepest gratitude have departed from the realistic scheme — *The Green Pastures* and *Yellow Jack*. Realism is practical and forceful. You cannot ask for a grimmer anatomy of death than *Mourning Becomes Electra* or a more exciting show than *Broadway*. But the dramatist who is aglow with spirit cannot get higher than tip-toe on the realistic stage. 'A poet soaring in the high region of his fancies, with his garland and singing robes about him', must invent a buoyant medium of expression.

From any long point of view it is childish to wonder that a man bred to physical labor should succeed where conscious artists have failed. Work does not terrify the laborer. Being a man confident of his strength he attacks a job with singleness of purpose. What makes *Within the Gates*, not merely a technical achievement, but a fantasy impregnated with the joy and terror of life, is the simplicity of Mr O'Casey's courage. He is a natural man. If the world were not a debased corner of the universe every man would be a natural being with nothing to fear and nothing to hide. But life on this ball spinning through the Milky Way is so twisted by false dogmas, vanity, greed and economic insecurity that a natural

* *The New York Times* (28 Oct. 1934).

man, like Walt Whitman or Sean O'Casey is a cosmic event. Life is astonishingly simple for a man who has no reservations. Without bragging or making disingenuous responses, he can say what he feels and believes, for he is free. No one can intimidate him or overpower him; no one can put him out of countenance. He is free to march forward in the direction of his genius; and he can even love his enemies if he wishes.

When Mr O'Casey left Dublin, after a tumultuous quarrel with the directors of the Abbey Theatre who would not produce *The Silver Tassie*, he settled in London and fell under the spell of Hyde Park. In that garden and open-air forum, where the quacks and the prophets rub shoulders, the spiritual drama of England is played every day of the year. We have nothing quite like it here, although Central Park, Union Square, the Battery and the open piers are pungent with humanity. But to the poet, in whose eye the beauty liveth, Hyde Park is a microcosm of modern England. Life saunters aimlessly by — love, fear, terror, lust, devotion to God, and unending processional of denials and affirmations. Having his mind open Mr O'Casey has relished the whole pageant and sweetened it with the natural love he had for things that grow, sing and are alive.

Whether *Within the Gates* is a fantasy or masque or either I'm sure I don't know, nor does Mr O'Casey. Once he lived next door to Milton's cottage.[2] 'Beyond Milton's cottage is O'Casey's bungalow,' he use to announce to his friends with a ripple of Irish humor. Perhaps there is a touch of Milton in the play. Certainly there is a strong infiltration of the full-blooded Shakespearean speech, and a few hints of classic drama, expressionism and *The Shephard's Calendar*. In four scenes with a common setting, representing Spring, Summer, Autumn and Winter, Mr O'Casey presents the myriad folk of Hyde Park in pursuit of the glories of being alive. Some of it is grandly comic, like the interminable arguments about God and atheism. Some of it is satiric, like the Bishop's elephantine truckling to the common people. Some of it is terrifyingly tragic, like the chorus of the down-and-outs. None of the characters is an individual. They are all symbolic of various aspects of life. Although *Within the Gates* has only the most trifling story, it is essentially a drama of life in opposition to death. Those who are most gloriously alive in it are always within earshot of death. You soon know where Mr O'Casey's sympathies lie. He showers his poetic riches upon those who live fearlessly —

upon The Dreamer, in fact, whom I wish Mr O'Casey had labeled
The Poet. When the cringing, lamenting chorus of the down-
and-outs reaches out hungrily for another corpse, The Dreamer
drives them back with a song:

> Way for the strong and the swift and the fearless;
> Life that is stirr'd with the fear of its life, let it die;
> Let it sink down, let it die, and pass from our vision forever.
> Sorrow and pain we shall have, and struggle unending;
> We shall weave courage with pain, and fight through the
> struggle unending.
> Way for the strong and the swift and the fearless;
> Life that is weak with the terror of life, let it die;
> Let it sink down, let it die, and pass from our vision forever!

When *Within the Gates* was published last Winter I did not
foresee the lyric beauty of the acting production. If Charles
Morgan and George Jean Nathan[3] had not admired it so keenly I
should have been willing to conclude that the tumultuous author
of *Juno and the Paycock* and *The Plough and the Stars* had
strayed completely beyond his depth. But the buoyant
performance now on view at the National is the finest evidence of
what they and he foresaw in this great play. That tremulous
production proves that *Within the Gates* is not a literary piece,
but theatre incarnate, not to be savored apart from the stage.
The ballet dancing is lamentably patronizing and should be
eliminated. But the music, which is as pure as a folk dance or a
troubadour's love song, and James Reynolds' sense of living color
in the costumes and settings, and the acting and Lillian Gish and
Bramwell Fletcher, have lifted the magnificence of the spirit out
of the bare text. Once upon a time Yeats wrote of Synge: 'The
ordinary student of drama will not find anywhere in *The Well of
the Saints* that excitement of will in the presence of attainable
advantage which he is accustomed to think the natural stuff of
drama.' Something of the same sort applies to *Within the Gates*.
Mr O'Casey is not trying to impose his will on ours. Sitting in
Hyde Park he has found life good, in spite of distant alarms, and
he has transmuted his thoughts into song, dance and drama. 'Our
mother, the earth, is a maiden again, young, fair, and a maiden
again,' his chorus sings when the curtains part. Full of the
common joy, O'Casey has uttered some, like one of the noblest of
his predecessors.

NOTES

1. For cast list and other production details, see Atkinson's article of 23 October 1934, pp. 60–2.
2. O'Casey lived at Hillcrest, Chalfont St Giles, Buckinghamshire from October 1934 to September 1938. Milton's cottage was only a short distance from Hillcrest.
3. George Jean Nathan, *Vanity Fair* (New York), (Jan. 1934) pp. 42, 56, and Charles Morgan, '*Within the Gates*: Further Thoughts on Sean O'Casey's Recently Shown Play', *The New York Times* (25 Feb. 1934) sect. 9, p. 3.

Boston Secedes from the Universe*

Up there on Olympus the gods must be snickering to themselves. The bureaucrats of Boston, who lived undefiled through an invasion of *Point Valaine*, have refused *Within the Gates* permission to sing and dance in Tremont Street. Like one of the characters in Mr O'Casey's masque, they insist upon 'turning the song of life into a mea maxima culpa.' For the traditional genius of censors is to make fools of themselves by discovering low motives in decentminded plays and by running to cover when a dramatist ventures to redeem the theatre from commonness.

When Mr O'Neill's *Strange Interlude*, which was crowned with the Pulitzer Prize, set out for Boston several years ago the cultured politicians of that metropolis entertained the world and enraged all intelligent Bostonians by refusing to license it. Bigotry that is pompous in manner and petty in mentality is generally diverting. Since then the world has discovered that industry, the stock market and international polity are more fatal to the health of the nation than dramatic stages; and being engrossed by the urgencies of the depression the world had almost forgotten Boston's last flare of grandmotherly temperament. To the other signs of returning economic confidence add the spectacle of the Boston censorship. With uncanny chuckle-headedness it has picked the

* First published under the title, 'Thundering in the Index: In Banning *Within the Gates* Boston Withdraws from Universe again — Religion of O'Casey's Play', *The New York Times* (27 Jan. 1935).

wrong play to misconstrue. The bigwigs of Boston are again with-
drawing from the universe. 'Take your elegant and perfum'd soul
out of the stress and strain, the horrid cries, the noisy laugh of
life, an' go out into the sun, an' pick the yellow primroses!' says
one of the characters in *Within the Gates*. The censors of Boston
now feel sufficiently safe to accept that scornful advice. Egged on
by a handful of misguided clergymen, they feel justified in
banning the most religious play the modern drama has produced.

There is this much to be said for the Boston art students: they
are not trivial. Before discharging their thunderbolts they wait for
something big to come along. When Noel Coward's drama of lust
in the West Indies was raising the temperature of Boston play-
goers the censors realized that it was not one of his most formidable works and were, accordingly, not upset by the dankness of its
sensuality. Although *Point Valaine* is a true portrait of the corruption of moral fibre in the hot climates, its truth lacks the
universality of Mr O'Casey's poem in praise of the glory of being
alive. For the little men with morbid minds who set themselves up
as the custodians of public taste object to the stage most seriously
when it stops giggling and sniggering for a moment and sings of
life with the religious fervor of poetic imagery. Mr O'Casey's rank
offense is that he has dared write of the spirit and employ the
blunt, sinewy language of the King James Bible and the Elizabethans. Censors tremble in the presence of a man who is fully
alive; he is a challenge to their terror; he reminds them of the
feebleness of their grasp on life. When *Leaves of Grass* appeared
Emerson was the only Bostonian who understood the significance
of Walt Whitman's vitality, and even Emerson felt uncomfortable
about it.

Although New York is no paragon of civic virtue, the fathers of
the city have a rough-hewn respect for the freedom of the arts.
Some years ago when Tammany was chiefly engrossed in the
pastime of swindling the taxpayers it performed the penitent
gesture of blowing a police whistle at *The Captive* and *Maya*; and
when the investigations into political depravity became alarming
Tammany wished very much that a certain melodrama based on
those scandals could be discreetly kept off the boards. Occasion-
ally the constabulary backs a patrol-wagon up to a burlesque
house today and arrests the girls and mountebanks who are
cheating the customers for a manager's fee. But it is impossible to
conceive of Mayor La Guardia's joining the Philistines or suffer-

ing the Philistines to hold his city up to ridicule by imposing their artistic myopia upon a free citizenry.

In addition to being a political firebrand, the Mayor has the artistic sensibilities of a man of emotional temperament. He believes in the beauty of art as well as the nutriment of bread. Probably he would not fix his personal cachet on a good many of the theatre's exhibitions; no one who is high-minded or fastidious could. But under the present regime of city management, stupid little obscenities, like *Slightly Delirious*, are almost certain to die without ruining anything except the cash drawer, and serious attempts to portray human degradation, like *Tobacco Road* and *Point Valaine*, enjoy the privilege of being discussed as studies of life. I hold no brief for the purity of the theatre, which is always threatened by a few playwrights and managers with the minds of brothel keepers. But I submit that the theatre as a forum for discussion and revelation is best served by city fathers who are not alarmed by ideas that are new to them. Having been branded as smutty and anti-religious by a few willful politicians and terrified clerics in Boston, *Within the Gates* has now returned to New York, where even the people who dislike it know that neither of those charges is true.

When the Catos of the Bay State denounce *Within the Gates* as an anti-religious play, they mean something less far-reaching. They mean that it is anti-church, which is at any rate partly true. The Bishop in Mr O'Casey's play truckles to the poor and lowly; although he is not without sin himself, he is unable to cope with the vast tumult of life that drifts and roars through a common city park. Many churchmen share that opinion; and certainly the Boston censors lend weight to Mr O'Casey's critical point of view; they could hardly discover a more sensational way to prove his point, and to make a prophet of a playwright. Although he is damned by literal-minded ecclesiasts and commissioners in Boston, he has also been blessed by Roman Catholic and Episcopalian clergymen in the East for the exaltation of the religious spirit in his play. For the religious spirit is grander than churches, which endeavor humbly to serve it. The religious spirit is faith in God, and that impulse runs fervently through all the scenes of Mr O'Casey's masque and fantasy. It is the symbol of life and courage; it is the music of the earth. Lest any one have any doubt of his buoyant faith, he wrote it into the concluding chant:

Way for the strong and the swift and the fearless:
Life that is stirr'd with the fear of its life, let it die;
Let it sink down, let it die, and pass from our vision forever.

Incidentally, let that serve also as a creed for censors.

The Play*

RETURN OF THE ABBEY THEATRE PLAYERS IN O'CASEY'S *THE PLOUGH AND THE STARS*

After devoting two seasons to their private affairs, the Abbey
Theatre Players have come rolling into town again. Joy be unto
them and us. Last evening they opened their day-to-day repertory
at the Golden Theatre with a revival of Sean O'Casey's *The
Plough and the Stars*,[1] which was first performed here by another
troupe in 1927. After an interval of seven years, it still looks like a
masterpiece in the raffish production of the Abbey company and
still sounds like a masterpiece in the lilt of their voices. It did seem
to this herald last evening that some of the players, particularly
Barry Fitzgerald and Michael J. Dolan, had not yet adjusted their
voices to the spaces of the Golden Theatre, and that Mr Fitzgerald had not yet made the proper compromise between brogue
and intelligibility. Some of his most pungent lines were tangled in
his bristling mustache. It is well to get criticism done with in the
opening paragraph, for these lines are intended as a jubilant
review and a cordial greeting to one of the grandest band of
actors in the world today.

Unless memory is at fault, some of the Irish patriots in Dublin
tried last summer to prevent their playing the O'Casey drama
here this season. Now the government is absolved from blame
with a line on the program: 'The Abbey Theatre receives an
annual subsidy from the government of the Irish Free State; the
government does not interfere with, nor is it responsible for, the
theatre's repertory of plays.' The note of caution is well taken. For

* *The New York Times* (13 Nov. 1934).

Mr O'Casey's grim and biting play, with its riotous surface comedy, does not flatter the gallantry of the members of the Citizen Army who poured out their blood on the streets of Dublin in 1916. Being full of humanity, Mr O'Casey hates warfare and bloodshed. He writes down the revolution as nothing nobler than folly. His insurgents are not motivated by heroism. They are either vain or excitable men, intoxicated by words and stupid oratory. Although he is no wit, his iconoclasm is bitter and wounding.

What makes *The Plough and the Stars* no bit of special pleading but a racy folk drama is the vigor and dash of the characterizations and the comic twist to the lines. In the streets outside, the men are marching or the orators are roaring or the soldiers are firing. But inside the tenements and pubs the ebullient tenement dwellers behave like turbulent children. Amid the squalor of poverty they argue furiously with works they do not understand and lance into shrewish combat. What lusty characters! Mr O'Casey lets them have it out of his knowledge of and his love and pity for his countrymen.

Probably there could be a funnier actor than Barry Fitzgerald, but probably we mortals will never see one. His Fluther Good, with his ignorant piety and general belligerence, is uproarious comic acting. Under Mr Fitzgerald's dreary, wretched make-up is a rich comic spirit that can translate such plain words as 'I don' know, I don' know' into the stoutest of low comedy lines. If Mr Fitzgerald has an absurdly enjoyable time playing the part of Fluther Good, it is only fair to add that the audience shares his relish and enthusiasm. It looks like caricature to us, but it is not. It is inspired projection of groundling character.

Not that Mr Fitzgerald plunders the show. For low comedy, May Craig as the charwoman and Maureen Delany are quite as funny and considerably more articulate with their lines. In the anxious parts of Nora and Jack Clitheroe, Eileen Crowe and F.J. McCormick play like honest actors, and Michael J. Dolan is excellent as the crackbrained Young Covey. W[illiam] O'Gorman catches little of the quality of Peter Flynn, who is the pasteboard soldier; his acting is still inexperienced. But that is the only foggy patch in the clear horizon of a lively, bubbling performance. The Abbey Players have not only gifts but integrity.

Since the time when he was writing *Juno and the Paycock* and *The Plough and the Stars* Mr O'Casey has turned his back on realism and written *Within the Gates*. The comparison is vivid, now that two of his plays are simultaneously visible representing two styles of craftsmanship.[2] Although *The Plough and the Stars* is firm, muscular, overpowering drama, fashioned out of living realities, it seems to this theatregoer that *Within the Gates* is much the finer piece of work. It has greater compass, a more buoyant spirit and a more sensitive dramatic texture. The comparison is really a contrast: *Within the Gates* and *The Plough and the Stars* differ completely in motive. But what Mr O'Casey has accomplished in the long period since he wrote *The Plough and the Stars* is beautifully mirrored in *Within the Gates*.

NOTES

1. The Abbey Theatre Players presented by Elbert A. Wickes at the Golden Theatre, 12 November 1934. Total performances: 13.

Cast:		
	Commandant Jack Clitheroe	F.J. McCormick
	Nora Clitheroe	Eileen Crowe
	Peter Flynn	William O'Gorman
	The Young Covey	Michael J. Dolan
	Fluther Good	Barry Fitzgerald
	Bessie Burgess	Maureen Delany
	Mrs Gogan	May Craig
	Mollser	Aideen O'Connor
	Captain Brennan	Denis O'Dea
	Lieut. Langan	Una Wright
	Rosie Redmond	Frolie Mulhern
	A Bargain	P.J. Carolan
	A Voice	P.J. Carolan
	Corporal Stoddard	P.J. Carolan
	Sergeant Tinley	Arthur Shields

2. *Within the Gates* was playing at the National Theatre at the same time.

The Play*

SEAN O'CASEY'S *JUNO AND THE PAYCOCK* ACTED BY THE ABBEY THEATRE TROUPE

When the whole world is in a terrible state of chassis it is a temptation for a man to slip off and see the Abbey Theatre Players in Sean O'Casey's *Juno and the Paycock*, which turned up at the Ambassador last evening.[1] For this bitter cartoon of Dublin in the evil times of 1922 is one of the lustiest pieces of tatterdemalion literature in our language — a low comedy antic and a courageous indictment of muddle. Some glorious actors have shuffled and sung their way through the leading parts of the tenement dwellers of Dublin in this play. Many of the lines still echo inspired voices. Although P.J. Carolan is now playing shiftless 'Captain' Boyle with good humor and thorough understanding, his literal acting is no match for the comic genius of Barry Fitzgerald, whose querulous voice and pompous futility used to set the whole theatre rocking when he was strutting on the stage. Mr Carolan will perhaps forgive us for mourning a great piece of acting. A part and an actor are not often so perfectly mated as were 'Captain' Boyle and Fitzgerald.

It would be easier to become reconciled to the loss of Fitzgerald if one could feel that the rest of the company still had fresh enthusiasm for Mr O'Casey's first successful play. Even without their great comic spirit they are good players whose gentleness and devotion have won many friends in this city. But there is no blinking the fact that their *Juno and the Paycock* needs vigorous re-direction. The performance has subsided into slovenliness of detail. Little excesses of detail, like Maureen Delany's mugging in her song number, have crept in to delight the customers rather than to convey the play. Being loosely written, *Juno* needs a firm hand in the staging to evoke the grim contrast between the tenement folk comedy and the tragic intrusion of civil war. Perhaps it needs a new performance idea altogether with a reassignment of positions and a more astringent interpretation of the lines. This play has gone to the well of the Abbey Players once too often. Not that *Juno and the Paycock* is thrown away by the visiting Dubli-

---

* *The New York Times* (7 Dec. 1937).

ners. F.J. McCormick's slippery Joxer is still a richly amusing study in tattered treachery. Although Eileen Crowe's tongue may not be stinging enough, her Juno is a good piece of acting, and Maureen Delany's neighborly Maisie Madigan is good when she is not truckling to the audience in the comedy scenes. But the Abbey Theatre Players have been nudging light comedy around so long that they have lost the strength to pitch vigorously into a big drama. Mr O'Casey's emotions and thoughts are so violent that he would not recognize them in a fatigued performance of his play.

NOTES

1. Performed by the Abbey Theatre in association with the Messrs. Shubert at the Ambassador Theatre, 6 December 1937. Total performances: 8

Cast:	
Captain Jack Boyle	P.J. Carolan
Juno Boyle	Eileen Crowe
Johnny Boyle	Arthur Shields
Mary Boyle	Aideen O'Connor
'Joxer' Daly	F.J. McCormick
Maisie Madigan	Maureen Delany
'Needle' Nugent	Michael J. Dolan
Mrs Tancred	May Craig
Jerry Devine	Denis O'Dea
Charles Bentham	Joseph Linnane
An Irregular	Austin Meldon
A Sewing Machine Woman	Frolie Mulhern
A Vendor	Una Wright
Neighbors, Furniture Removal Men, Second Irregular	

The Play*

BARRY FITZGERALD, SARA ALLGOOD RESUME ORIGINAL PARTS IN *JUNO AND THE PAYCOCK*

Although Barry Fitzgerald and Sara Allgood appeared in the original stormy performance of *Juno and the Paycock* in Dublin

* *The New York Times* (17 Jan. 1940).

in 1924, they have never appeared together in New York until
now.[1] Miss Allgood played Juno in the troupe of Irish players that
brought the O'Casey drama here in 1927.[2] Barry Fitzgerald
played Captain Boyle with the visiting Abbey Theatre company
in 1932 and 1934.[3] By happy chance they are now free to play
together again in a revival put on at the Mansfield last evening.
The performance as a whole needs considerable sharpening of
mood to convey the tragic bitterness that hangs over this savage
portrait of the Irish revolution. But count it as a dispensation to
have two such glorious actors as Miss Allgood and Mr Fitzgerald
in immortal parts that suit them. They are both in fine fettle just
now.

Probably Mr Fitzgerald will never have a richer part. Captain
Boyle can hardly be overdrawn. Mr Fitzgerald's notion of this
raffish tenement charlatan of Dublin is fantastically comic.
Dressed in wrinkled rags that cling uncertainly to his portly
figure, a huge belt carelessly buckled around his waist, a squalid
cap at an angle on his head, Captain Boyle is stern and pompous
on the surface and all bluff underneath. Mr Fitzgerald's general
unintelligibility is plainly a fault in any sort of acting. But in the
light of his comic intonations it is a fault that seems less grievous
than it is. For Mr Fitzgerald's tightly-drawn face is an essential
part of his portrait — querulous and alarmed by turns; and his
voice plays tunes on the character. Sometimes it rises to the
singsong of public speaking. Captain Boyle is a part that Mr Fitzgerald enjoys. He has played it so long that he has filled out all the
lines of O'Casey's racy drawing. It is one of the theatre's modern
masterpieces.

Although the part of Juno is less spectacular, Miss Allgood's
playing of it is a masterpiece also. Juno is the woman who takes all
the responsibility in this harum-scarum family. She cannot preen
herself as extravagantly as her shiftless husband. But Miss Allgood's hot-tempered playing reaches down all through Mr
O'Casey's drama and stirs up some of the ground swell of feeling
that should be there. In Miss Allgood's acting Juno is a strong
character — swift of foot and mind, with the remnants of middle-
class respectability coming instinctively to life on social occasions.

A tatterdemalion in her dress and a shrew in speech, she is a
mother in the protection she instinctively gives to her children,
and she never forgets to straighten her hair and smooth down her
apron when she answers a knock on the door. The tragic scenes at

the close of the play Miss Allgood acts with an anguish that gets closer to the heart of O'Casey's drama than anything else in the performance. She may well be proud of the honesty and skill of this bustling portrait of a mother against whom the black world she knows has pitilessly conspired.

As a performance of the play as a whole this revival is partly inadequate. Arthur Shields, who acts the shifty 'Joxer' satisfactorily, has not succeeded in his role as director in bringing the whole play into focus. The comedy runs away with O'Casey's mordant indictment of the Dublin revolution. The black cloud of doom does not hang far enough down into the heedless life of the Boyle family. There is more pathos than bitterness in the second-act curtain. Aideen O'Connor plays a very good Mary Boyle, but the rest of the company is never better than mediocre. There is a fearless thrust of criticism in O'Casey that only partly comes through the surface of this revival. Although Mr Shields knows the play intimately, he has staged it at top speed and has not had time to beat the performance into shape. Perhaps he can still make the rest of it more worthy of the two grand actors who are in it. What Mr Fitzgerald and Miss Allgood are doing deserves a triumphant performance of a wonderful play.

NOTES

1. Revived by Edward Choate and Arthur Shields in association with Robert Edmond Jones at the Mansfield Theatre, 16 December 1940. Total performances: 105

Cast:	
Mary Boyle	Aideen O'Connor
Juno Boyle	Sara Allgood
Johnny Boyle	Harry Young
Jerry Devine	Thomas Dillon
Captain Jack Boyle	Barry Fitzgerald
'Joxer' Daly	Arthur Shields
A Sewing Machine Vendor	Irish Whitney
A Coal Block Vendor	William Stone
Charlie Bentham	Lucian Self
Mrs Maisie Madigan	Grania O'Malley
Mrs Tancred	Effie Shannon
'Needle' Nugent	Hale Norcross
An Irregular Mobilizer	Charles Keenan
Furniture Removal Man	Byron Russell
Asst. Furniture Removal Man	Jack Graham
Neighbors	Hancy O'Grady

George O'Regan
Harry Selby

Staged by Arthur Shields
Setting by Robert Edmond Jones
2. See pp. 43–6, Atkinson's column, 'The Play: Again the Irish Players' (20 Dec. 1927).
3. See pp. 53–5, Atkinson's column, 'Tatterdemalions of Dublin in *Juno and the Paycock*, (20 Oct. 1932).

*Juno and the Paycock**

Some day, somewhere, some young people will be thinking enviously of the time when Sean O'Casey was writing mighty plays and Barry Fitzgerald and Sara Allgood were around to act them. The first half of the twentieth century will seem like a golden age when it is over. At the moment when things occur it is the fashion to take them casually. A revival of *Juno and the Paycock*, with Mr Fitzgerald as Captain Boyle and Miss Allgood as his valiant wife, may seem like only an interesting interlude in the midst of a languid season.[1] But the O'Casey drama of civil war in Ireland in 1922 ranks with the finest work in modern English, and Mr Fitzgerald and Miss Allgood play it like inspired actors. To people of moderate temperament this paragraph of introduction may seem to be in too high a key. But it proceeds from sober conviction and it is intended to arouse theatregoers to realization of one thing that is going on under their noses. The time to appreciate notable occasions is when they are happening.

Among the things for which we should always be duly grateful is the English language. It is a thing not only of beauty but of force and passion. It is the genius of our civilization. Chaucer, Shakespeare, the translators of the King James Bible, and Milton have endowed it with fervor and grandeur. In its purest state, it is a simple language with tremendous muscle and pliability, and it can encompass anything real or imaginative. No man ever had a thought that the English language could not express and share

* *The New York Times* (28 Jan. 1940).

intimately with English and American people.

Mr O'Casey's schooling in Ireland was sketchy at best, partly because of his mother's poverty and partly because of a sickness of his eyes. But by some uncanny instinct he learned his English from Shakespeare and the Bible which are the treasure houses of our speech; and he seasoned it in the fiery talk he heard around the pubs and street corners of Dublin. His English is not self-consciously literary. Usually he does not ornament his prose. He does not select words fastidiously. Even when he is writing deliberately in the classical tradition, as in *Within the Gates*, he is spare and blunt. When he is hotly aroused by the spectacle of rancorous stupidity, as in *Juno and the Paycock*, he writes in the idiom of common people with superb drive and buoyancy.

Most of *Juno and the Paycock* is mordant comedy, gusty and slatternly in manner, but contemptuous in spirit. We can take it with more equanimity than the Irish because we are far removed from the scene and the angry incidents that produced it. To the unsuspecting theatregoer Mr O'Casey may seem to be making a jig of the Paycock's empty swagger and Joxer's treacherous fawning. But when Mr O'Casey is ready to comment on the ignorant squalor of the scene he has been sketching, the heat and lift of his writing are unparalleled in modern English. Juno has the great speech near the close of the last act. The circumstances are poignant. Her lazy dissembling husband has let her down for years; her silly daughter has been ruined by a snob who has deserted her; her sniveling boy has just been murdered by the insurgents. Everything has collapsed around her. As she goes out to claim the limp body of her son, her parting speech is a cry of anguish that ought to leave a permanent scar on the complacence of the world: 'What was the pain I suffered, Johnny, bringin' you into the world to carry to your cradle to the pains I'll suffer carryin' you out o' the world to bring you to your grave! Mother o' God, Mother o' God, have pity on us all! Blessed Virgin, where were you when me darlin' son was riddled with bullets, when me darlin' son was riddled with bullets? Sacred heart o' Jesus, take away our hearts o' stone and give us hearts o' flesh! Take away this murd-herin' hate, an' give us Thine own eternal love!'

No one can speak these lines with the tragic loneliness that Miss Allgood imparts to them. For they come as a climax to a superb evening of acting and they are an integral part of the character she has busily created from the rise of the curtain. Her acting is not showy. Juno is the plain foundation of the play — the tired, bustling, tenacious mother of a heedless family, doing her duty loyally according to her standards of decency. Ignorant as she is, she knows how worthless and hopeless the battle of life is without intelligence to direct it. Nothing deceives her. Although her temper is quick, her patience is inexhaustible. Amid the dinginess of the scene Miss Allgood manages wonderfully to convey the enlightened character of this slum drudge and to suggest its universal dimensions; and she has the technical skill necessary to make it count across the footlights.

As the Paycock, Mr Fitzgerald's richly comic acting in a vein of realism is something to be cherished for a lifetime. It is flamboyant and full of comic daring. Mr Fitzgerald is, I think, unnecessarily inarticulate. Despite the tightness of his speech, his acting is irresistible. For the variety of his intonations, from snappish ill temper to the rolling periods of pompousness, describes the character by sound alone, and his extravagant strut is immensely funny. To be ideal this revival needs the parasitical Joxer of F. J. McCormick, and some of the other parts could be better played. But Mr Fitzgerald and Miss Allgood in one of O'Casey's three great plays is golden age enough for one New York Winter.

NOTES

1. For production details see pp. 74–7, Atkinson's column, 'The Play' (17 Jan. 1940).

*The Silver Tassie**

INTERPLAYERS' REVIVAL IS SIGNAL SERVICE

No one is angrily denouncing Sean O'Casey's *The Silver Tassie* today. The young people who dub themselves the Interplayers have been acting it for seven weeks in their air-cooled theatre at

* *The New York Times* (4 Sept. 1949).

Carnegie Hall; and most people recognize it as a vigorous and biting drama about the horrors of war by a fiery and gifted dramatist.[1]

Twenty-one years ago and again in 1935 it raised the bloodheat of Dublin to the boiling point, and started a whole series of sparring, punches and blows. Rejecting it for the Abbey Theatre, which owed its life to *Juno and the Paycock* and *The Plough and the Stars*, Yeats sorrowfully declared that *The Silver Tassie* had no theme and that Mr O'Casey was not interested in the war, and Mr O'Casey replied with a blast that must have singed the paper it was written on. The rejection of *The Silver Tassie* by the Abbey Theatre became one of the celebrated causes of the day.

When the Abbey Theatre magnanimously relented in 1935 and put on *The Silver Tassie*, Mr O'Casey's drama had a few friends, notably Robert Speaight. But the enemies were more numerous and clamorous than the friends. Mr O'Casey's broadside against war was denounced as obscene, revolting, outrageous and hysterical. Since Dublin was then populated almost exclusively by bitter partisans, the acidulous comments on *The Silver Tassie* were not exactly judicious.

From the ideal point of view it is not a wholly satisfactory play because it arbitrarily introduces one act of expressionism in the midst of a realistic play, and not everything in the expressionistic act is as intelligible as the rest. But Mr O'Casey might cite as precedent the enigmatic battlescenes of Shakespeare, who also was unable to fit the sweeping thunder of war into the neat confines of the stage. Not having taken the precaution to study under Strindberg and Ibsen, Shakespeare was a diffuse writer, too.

Since the time when Mr O'Casey wrote *The Silver Tassie*, something very crucial to the drama has been happening: theatregoers have acquired considerable agility of mind. The trend of the drama has been away from naturalism toward flexibility of style, conspicuously so in the works of Thornton Wilder and Tennessee Williams and most recently in Arthur Miller's *Death of a Salesman*. The form of *The Silver Tassie* is accordingly more congenial than it was when Mr O'Casey broke with his previous work and composed this drama in a more subjective manner.

On the fact of it, *The Silver Tassie* was written by an Irishman who had Irish music ringing in his head. The polyglot performance by the Interplayers loses the ecstasy of the writing. This is a serious fault that cannot be politely ignored, for it robs the play of a good deal of simple poetry. But sound and discerning direction often provides a sturdy staff that an ill-assorted company can hang on to, and that is what has happened here. Al Saxe, the director, knows what the play is about and has given the performance solid architecture. Whatever their individual abilities may be, the actors know what they are doing.

Memories of performances twenty years ago are unreliable, since standards of judgement are not fixed. But unless memory is deceptive, Mr Saxe's direction is more coherent than the direction of the Irish Players' production of *The Silver Tassie* at the Old Greenwich Village Theatre in October, 1929. Mr Saxe has not lost the thread of Harry Heegan's disastrous career that runs unevenly through the robustious comic scenes, the expressionistic masque and the haunted festivity of the last act. Although the pattern of *The Silver Tassie* is intricate and impulsive, Mr Saxe has assimilated and mastered it.

Specifically, the play is about Harry Heegan, a fabulous football player and the hero of his club, who is wounded in the war and condemned to the life of a wheel-chair invalid for the rest of his days. In the tumultuous character of Harry Heegan, played with complete understanding, especially in the last act, by Jack Palance, Mr O'Casey has represented the agonizing human tragedy of war.

But since he is naturally a writer of extraordinary dimensions, *The Silver Tassie* is much more than the drama of an individual. Mr O'Casey has, among other things, the Shakespearean gift for writing low comedy. Beginning with the immortal Joxer and Captain Boyle in *Juno and the Paycock*, he has created a whole gallery of Shakespearean fools — energetic, loquacious, prejudice-ridden mortals who like to talk big and wonder about great subjects. Shakespeare got his characters out of the Stratford country. Mr O'Casey has taken his out of the city of Dublin.

Happily, *The Silver Tassie* begins with the comic altercations of two shifty, roisterous ne'er-do-wells. In these racy characters Mr O'Casey catches the conviviality, treachery, ignorance, belligerence, fanaticism and love of brave words that he has written about before. Approximating the tangy Irish speech as nearly as they can, Henri Beckman and Gene Dow play these characters with a kind of dazed gusto that is continuously funny. Nancy Stiber and Anna Berger also do well by the parts of two women who are close to the chiselers in spirit and locale.

No doubt there could be better performances of *The Silver Tassie* than the one we are having this summer. But the plain fact is that there are and have been none better or as good here. The Interplayers, who trouble the unions by not being able to pay salaries to actors, have brought to life a trenchant drama by an indomitable writer who is incomparably gifted. That is a signal service to the community. 'I love the way I imagine the Greeks wrote (from English translations) and I love the way I know the Elizabethans wrote,' Mr O'Casey says, 'and I am anxious and eager to make use of both in the things I try to write.'[2] He is ambitious. On the evidence of *The Silver Tassie*, he is entitled to be.

NOTES

1. By 'Interplayers' at Carnegie Hall, 21 July to 9 October 1949. Total performances: 80

Cast:		
Sylvester Heegan	Henri Beckman
Simon Norton	Gene Dow
Susie Monican	Nancy Stiber
Mrs Foran	Anna Berger
Mrs Heegan	Elsa Fried
Teddy Foran	Fred Porcelli
Barney Bagnal	Bill Weaver**
Jessie Taite	Anne Meara
Harry Heegan	Jack Palance
The Croucher	Ben M. Hammer
1st Soldier	Stefan Gierasch
2nd Soldier	Dennis McCarthy
3rd Soldier	Gerrit Walberg
4th Soldier	Roy M. Shuman
5th Soldier	James Alpe
6th Soldier	Leo Levenda
Visitor	John Clark
Corporal	Louis Criss
Staff Wallah	Maurice Edwards
Surgeon Forby Maxwell	John Denny
Sister	Francis Freeman

Directed by Al Saxe

2. Quote from O'Casey's letter to Atkinson, April 1939.

** Later known as Dennis Weaver, television star of 'Gunsmoke' and 'McCloud' series.

Case of O'Casey*

Although none of the New York or London commercial managers puts Sean O'Casey's dramas on the stage, his publishers continue to put them in print. The London house of Macmillan has recently published the second installment of the *Collected Plays*, and the New York branch of Macmillan has scheduled them for Oct. 2 here. In addition to the plays already published in single volumes, the *Collected Plays* include new ones in which Mr O'Casey humorously belabors some of the sins he despises most.

'Hall of Healing' portrays the heartlessness, incompetence and egotism of the administration of a Dublin dispensary for the poor — a topic Mr O'Casey can develop out of personal memories. 'Bedtime Story' is a farce about prudery and hypocrisy; and 'Time to Go' is a morality play about covetousness. These are one-act plays, set in Ireland. They are peopled with the sort of racy-tongued, combative, bigoted characters Mr O'Casey loves to write about — his scorn for their ignorance and duplicity tempered with his affection for their native vitality.

Mr O'Casey's quiet devotion to the composition of new dramas is a notable example of intestinal fortitude. There has not been a professional production of a new play by him on Broadway since *Within the Gates* in 1934. There have been very few professional productions anywhere in the world. *Cock-a-Doodle Dandy* has been available for production for two years, but the only professional production it has had anywhere was in Dallas under the direction of Margo Jones.[1]

Almost any other dramatist would be paralyzed by bitterness over such a bleak record. But Mr O'Casey appears to be unaffected by this wearing experience. Living in the country in Devon with his family, he keeps pegging away at the profession he likes — enjoying considerable fame around the world, receiving pilgrimages from admirers and inquiries from students, scribbling at the successive volumes of his autobiography, which is the finest achievement of his latter-day life, but receiving no encouragement from the stage.

He has made no compromises; he has surrendered none of his pride, principle or good humor, and he makes no personal com-

---

* *The New York Times* (16 Sept. 1951).

plaints. Having decided to become a professional writer about
thirty years ago, he takes the thin now with as much grace as he
took the thick when the old Abbey Theatre was playing *Juno and
the Paycock* and *The Plough and the Stars.*

Although it is customary to denounce commercial managers
for obtuseness about works of original art, the fault at present is
not all theirs. Several commercial managers of taste would like
very much to produce *Cock-a-Doodle Dandy* if they knew how to
stage it. Theoretically, any genuine piece of dramatic literature
can be staged if a director can create an imaginative production
and find a cast of actors composed of geniuses.

Bob Lewis,[2] a gifted director with a record of several original
productions, thinks he knows how to go about translating this
comic fantasy into stage terms; and it would be wonderful if there
were a place, like the Anta series, where he could try. But the
form of the play raises difficulties. *Cock-a-Doodle Dandy* does not
have a tangible subject like the ones that animated Mr O'Casey's
fiery plays from the Dublin period. His genius is commonly recognized now, but the full-length plays he is writing in Devon are
difficult to assimilate into the theatre.

Among the plays included in the new collected series is *Purple
Dust,* which was written in 1945. It has never been produced on
Broadway, although it is a more practicable play than *Cook-a-
Doodle Dandy.* It is closer to both people and the theatre. Under
the robustiousness of the satiric comedy and behind the occasional scenes of fantasy, there is a tangible problem to deal with and
recognizable people to fool with.

This is the yarn of two fatuous Englishmen who, in a mood of
nostalgic sentimentality, try to restore an old Irish mansion and
embrace the simple life. The house and the situation provide a
sort of frame that holds the play together and gives it depth and
perspective. As the story develops, the local Irish folk take subtle
advantage of the English nabobs in a rough-and-tumble lark that
amusingly conveys Mr O'Casey's contempt for solemn humbug
and his relish for the human delights of living.

Purple Dust could not be cast over the telephone or staged
casually. It needs to be acted with flavor and gusto. When Mr
O'Casey first came into the theatre he had the priceless asset of a
great company of actors at the Abbey or recently from the Abbey
who knew his characters and could set them to dancing on the
stage. In a way, all his plays still assume the availability of com-

parable actors. People who remember the acting of Arthur Sinclair, Maire O'Neill, Sara Allgood, F.J. McCormick and Barry Fitzgerald can hear echoes of their wonderful playing in the dialogue Mr O'Casey is writing today.

With *The Silver Tassie* in 1929 and *Within the Gates* in 1934, Mr O'Casey deliberately took his departure from realism and tried to write plays with more imaginative incantation. His success with these two plays justifies his search after new forms. Those two plays, written under the spell of his Dublin years, are grand pieces of work for theatregoers with flexible attitudes towards the stage and spiritual perceptions. Both of them have subjects and people. But a re-reading of *Cock-a-Doodle Dandy* confirms an earlier impression that the subject is generalized and elusive and the characters people of one dimension. Even a great dramatist, like Mr O'Casey, needs the discipline of constant production in the theatre. No one can get along forever without the excitement of actors and audiences all furiously absorbed in the miracle of getting something of value said on the stage.

NOTES

1. At 'Theatre 50' in Dallas, Texas, 30 January 1950.
2. Theatre director at Yale University, New Haven, Connecticut.

At the Theatre*

THREE NEW ONE-ACT PLAYS BY SEAN O'CASEY ARE PUT ON BY AN OFF-BROADWAY GROUP OF ACTORS

Eighteen years having elapsed since a new O'Casey play was done in this town, a patron of the arts instinctively rises to attention when a new bill is announced. Some actors who admire the most invisible of our dramatists have put on three O'Casey one-act plays at Yugoslav-American Hall, 405 West Forty-first Street, where they opened last evening.[1]

* *The New York Times* (8 May 1952).

The plays were written a good many years ago, but they were not published until last autumn.[2] They are *Hall of Healing*, which expresses O'Casey's hatred of institutionalized charity; *Bedtime Story*, which expresses his hatred of prudery; and *Time to Go*, which expresses his hatred of greed.

These are three of his main themes and principles. But there is no way of evading the fact that the plays are inferior O'Casey. You would hardly suspect that the man who wrote them is also author of *Juno and the Paycock* and the most glorious autobiography written in our time, two volumes of which are yet to be published.

Although the actors and impresarios of the current bill have Mr O'Casey's best interests at heart, they are not doing him any great service on the stage. To judge by the performances of the first two pieces, the acting is frantically inadequate. Neither the director of the first two plays nor the actors who are in them have any sense of genre style for Irish drama. If there were no Equity actors among them, you would assume that they were amateurs, taking a fling at something for which they have little talent.

In short, the current enterprise leaves the O'Casey saga about where it stopped eighteen years ago, when *Within the Gates* made the author many friends and a number of enemies. Since then he has written five or six full-length dramas, most of them presenting difficult problems of performance. They need to be staged and acted exclusively by geniuses, preferably nurtured on the old sod and saturated in Yeats and Synge.

NOTES

1. World premiere, 7 May 1952. Presented by the Three Plays Company.

Cast:	*Hall of Healing*	
	Alleluia	Benedict MacQuarrie
	Old Woman	Osceola Archer
	Red Muffler	John McLiam
	Doctor	Gilbert Green
	Apothecary	Kenneth Manigault
	Jentree	Michael Lewin
	Black Muffler	Michael Howard
	Young Woman	Peggy Bannion
	Green Muffler	Robert Donley
	Lad	Ronald Hamilton
	Grey Shawl	Melanie York

Townspeople	Peadar Noonan
	Vita Cox
	Ted Rowan
	Liam Lenihan
	Toni Tonley
	Maurice Winters
Directed by	Joseph Papirofsky
	(Joe Papp)
Designed	May Callas

Bedtime Story

John Jo Mulligan	Robert Donley
Angela Nightingale	Anne Jackson
Daniel Halibut	John McLiam
Miss Mossie	Osceola Archer
Directed by	Joseph Papirofsky
	(Joe Papp)
Designed by	May Callas

Time to Go

Bull Farrell	Clifford Carpenter
Flagonson	Leonard Yorr
Young Man	Arnold Walton
Young Woman	Melanie York
Widda Machree	Adelaide Bean
Mrs Flagonson	Edith Wade
Barney O'Hay	John McLiam
Cousins	Michael Howard
Conroy	Stefan Gierasch
Kelly	William Marshall
Sergeant	John Regan
Directed by	Albert Lipton
Designed by	May Callas

The Playful Mr O'Casey*

THE BISHOP'S BONFIRE: A SAD PLAY WITHIN THE TUNE OF A POLKA

In the published version of *The Bishop's Bonfire*, the frontispiece is a reproduction of an oil portrait of Sean O'Casey by his son, Breon.[1] Even in black-and-white it is an excellent picture. The face is thin and stern, like that of a bishop disapproving of his flock. But Breon knows his father too well to be satisfied with surface appearances. Look a little closer and the face turns out to be full of kindness as well as strength. The sterness does not represent anger. It represents disappointment. The bishop wished that his flock were happier.

Described as 'A sad play within the tune of a polka,' *The Bishop's Bonfire* was acted in Dublin last February under the direction of Tyrone Guthrie.[2] It was a considerable event, hissed, booed and applauded by the partisans on both sides. Cherishing fond memories of the riots caused by *The Plough and the Stars* twenty-nine years ago, Mr O'Casey felt encouraged.

This is a play on Mr O'Casey's favorite theme — the ideals of joy and freedom crushed by the puritanism and covetousness of the church. In the present case the church is Roman Catholic, although it is probably fair to say that Mr O'Casey is anti-clerical in general. He thinks organized religion makes God forbidding. 'Merriment may be a way of worship,' one of his characters says. That is a basic law in the O'Casey canon.

He has expressed this law with more of his own joy and freedom in *Cock-a-Doodle Dandy*, a raffish fantasy that no one seems both willing and able to produce. In comparison with that Irish lark, *The Bishop's Bonfire* is too much like a tract imposed on the characters but not drawn out of them. They are Irish types who serve Mr O'Casey's purpose. But none of them has the fiery reality of Juno Boyle in *Juno and the Paycock* or of Captain Brennan in *The Plough and the Stars*. The characters do not grow out of the soil of Ireland. They come out of Mr O'Casey's mind.

As usual, the writing has gusto and the comic scenes are broad, for Mr O'Casey enjoys the incongruities of his Irish scenes, like

* *The New York Times* (11 Sept. 1955).

the rude Irish peasants who try to fit themselves into elegant situations. There is some of the hugger-mugger of Gogol's *The Inspector General* in the point of view of the play. Yet *The Bishop's Bonfire* is two or three steps removed from life — the steps that lead into the library.

NOTES

1. The painting was given to Robert Emmet Ginna, at present editor-in-chief of Little, Brown and Co. It was destroyed in a fire in 1974.
2. World premiere of the play at the Gaiety Theatre, Dublin, 28 February 1955.

Theatre: O'Casey at Yale*

COCK-A-DOODLE DANDY ON SCHOOL STAGE

Despite the problems inherent in the script, the Yale School of Drama has staged Sean O'Casey's *Cock-a-Doodle Dandy* in the refurnished University Theatre. The engagement, which opened Tuesday, will conclude on Saturday night.

The problems are the ones that Mr O'Casey has raised by the impulsiveness of his craftsmanship. For *Cock-a-Doodle Dandy* is an odd brew of realism and fantasy, low comedy and supernaturalism, burlesque and preaching — the whole thing warmed by Mr O'Casey's love of mankind.

Let it be said at once that *Cock-a-Doodle Dandy* is puzzling but always engrossing. And the production under the direction of Frank McMullan is lively and intelligent. A company of experienced professionals might give a finer group performance. For *Cock-a-Doodle Dandy* needs to be orchestrated not only in the use of voices but also in the use of bodies. Possibly it will turn out to be the sort of play that asks the theatre for a kind of wild, incantated beauty that the theatre cannot deliver. But these remarks are not intended to reflect on the quality of the Yale

* *The New York Times* (4 Nov. 1955).

performance. It has more strength and versatility than you would expect from actors who are still studying their craft.

Since *Cock-a-Doodle Dandy* was published in 1949, it has been acted at the Arena Theatre in Dallas and by the Emerson School in Boston. Although Robert Lewis, the director, has wanted to stage it on Broadway for a long time, he has never been able to finance a commercial production.

Mr O'Casey is working at his old theme. He blasts avarice and piety; he cheers joy and freedom. His principal symbol of negation is the parish priest, who is Roman Catholic in this instance, though Mr O'Casey's anti-clericalism is not exclusive. He is a man of God who hates religious dogma of all kinds. To see *Cock-a-Doodle Dandy* on the stage, however, is to realize that it is intended to portray life in Ireland generally. Mr O'Casey's little world in an Irish provincial garden with prejudice, ignorance, superstition, hatred, fear and cruelty. The only characters of whom he approves are those who leave for a happier place. In this configuration of ideas one can perceive the symbol of Mr O'Casey's own experience. About thirty years ago he took off for England where he has been living in voluntary exile ever since. In a sense, *Cock-a-Doodle Dandy* is his summing-up. The tone is broadly comic. The point of view is bitter.

Cock-a-Doodle Dandy was written in exile not only from Ireland but also from the theatre. During the long years in which his new plays have been neglected by the commercial theatre, Mr O'Casey has been free from the disciplines of the stage. For an imaginative, eloquent, rebellious writer, this may not be a bad thing. But the more he is divorced from the theatre the more he ignores the usually accepted limitations of the stage. He lays enormous responsibility on the director and the actors for translating his free-hand style into theatrical terms. Presumably there is a way to act *Cock-a-Doodle Dandy* as spontaneously as he wrote it. But the company would have to be as virtuoso as a symphony orchestra or a ballet troupe.

Obviously, the graduate students at the Yale School of Drama are not on that ideal level yet. Individual performances are uniformly good, but the group performance is a little heavy and diffuse. Bernard Kukoff and Phil Bruns are roisterous and amusing as the two voluble Irishmen Mr O'Casey usually introduces into his plays, speaking a gaudy spurious prose above their station. Earle Rankin gives a forceful performance as the implacable clergyman.

Although the cast is long most of the acting is articulate and vigorous. Henry Lowenstein's setting of a house and garden shrewdly combines the mysticism and the reality that represent the spirit of the script. In this strange environment the performance solves the problems of supernaturalism surprisingly well.

Despite the inevitable inadequacies, this is a stimulating occasion. Some intelligent theatre people have got under the skin of a difficult script.

Theatre: Sean O'Casey*

After an absence of twenty-one years, Sean O'Casey has returned with a beautiful play, *Red Roses for Me*, which was acted at the Booth last evening.[1]

Since it was written twelve years ago, one can only wonder why it took so long to reach New York. Perhaps someone had to learn how to stage it. If so, John O'Shaughnessy is obviously the man. For he has staged it with humor and something approaching wonder in the last half of the evening. The melody of words is there; the pugnacious Irish comedy; the dreams of glory for Dublin, and finally the solemn church rites of the last act when a man of the people goes to his Maker, mourned by those who love him.

According to the program, the play is based on a strike in Dublin in 1913–14 that led to the 'bloody Easter Week Rising of 1916.' But as in all Mr O'Casey's latter-day plays, the real theme is the life of man — his valor, his joy, his love, his religious devotion, his loyalty and his belief in the future. Mr O'Casey has long since abandoned naturalistic drama for the poetry of mankind.

Some of *Red Roses for Me* will remind you of the raffish comedy of *Juno and the Paycock*. The gorgeous wrangles about

* *The New York Times* (29 Dec. 1955).

religion and patriotism in a tenement room, the drunken dance of words when men are quarreling over things beyond their understanding, the grotesque diversions into the absurd — are there in the first half of the evening as they were all through *Juno*.

There is some autobiography there, too. For the worker who spends his money on books and art and tries to learn the truth of the whole universe in one fell swoop is the O'Casey of half a century ago. And the patient mother who gets on with everyone and is never too worn to sit up with a sick neighbor is Mrs O'Casey, who had that mission in Sean's early life.

But most of all *Red Roses for Me* is a drama of verbal splendor. It wears the golden robe of words. In the course of the evening, the mood, even the nature of the play, changes — from homely comedy to an austere masque and then into religious devotion. But the flow of imagery and allusion runs on in a rich stream of words that glow with beauty and reveal the kindly wisdom of a man who has been in combat all his days but has never lost the purity of his faith in life. Rapturous writing comes naturally from his pen. He does not have to put phrases down on paper self-consciously.

All honor to the cast, as well as the director. For this is the sort of play that could easily have become a pose. But despite the luster of the style, the acting has its feet on the ground. Kevin McCarthy as the young lad who is trying to carry the world on his shoulders; Eileen Crowe, welcome to New York once more, giving a brave and tender performance as the mother; Joyce Sullivan as the maiden who loves a firebrand — play the central parts with softness, truth, and simplicity.

But the minor characters emerge in gusty performances that give the play its human scope. E.G. Marshall is very funny indeed as the belligerent Protestant. Eamon Flynn as the Roman Catholic and Casey Walters as the supercilious atheist are also amusing, and keep the battle of the dogmas salty and humorous.

In his designs for the scenery, Howard Bay may have insisted on too much literal detail, particularly for the first two acts. But the lighting is wonderfully evocative for the hymns to Dublin in the third act. There is a dance of joy in that scene, well designed by Anna Sokolow; and there is a lovely musical score by Edwin Finckel.

After the long absence it is wonderful to have another play by

Mr O'Casey that is original in style, pungent in humor, beautiful in its language and resolute in spirit. He always was a man.

NOTES

1. Produced by Gordon W. Pollock at the Booth Theatre, 28 December 1955.
   Total performances: 29

Cast:		
	Mrs Breydon	Eileen Crowe
	Ayamonn Breydon	Kevin McCarthy
	Eeada	Ann Dere
	Dympna	Katherine Hynes
	Finoola	Virginia Bosler
	First Neighbor	Farrell Pelly
	Second Neighbor	Page Johnson
	Third Neighbor	Vincent Dowling
	Sheila Moorneen	Joyce Sullivan
	Brennan o' the Moor	E.G. Marshall
	Sammy	David McDaniel
	Roory O'Balacaun	Eamon Flynn
	Mulcanny	Casey Walters
	Rev. E. Clinton	Michael Clarke Laurence
	First Railwayman	James C. Kelly
	Second Railwayman	Lou Frizzell
	Inspector Finglas	Shamus Locke
	Third Railwayman	David McDaniel
	Lounger	Paul Sanasardo
	Another Lounger	Jeff Duncan
	Old Woman	Beatrice Seckler
	Idle Woman	Judith Coy
	Lonely Man	David Gold
	Girl	Sandra Pine
	Another Girl	Eve Beck
	Drifter	Jack Moore
	Samuel	Whitford Kane
	Foster	Barry Macollum
	Dowzard	Jack McGraw
	Lamplighter	David Ryan

   Staged by John O'Shaughnessy
   Choreography by Anna Sokolow
   Scenery and Lighting by Howard Bay
   Costumes by Ballou
   General Stage Manager, William Weaver
   Stage Manager, Arthur Barklow
   Music by Edwin Finckel

Red Roses for Me*
O'CASEY'S BEAUTIFUL ODE TO THE GLORY OF LIFE

For about a quarter of a century Sean O'Casey has been writing dramas that have never been seen in New York. Until *Red Roses for Me* was put on at the Booth on Dec. 28,[1] no new full-length play by him had been acted here since *Within the Gates* in 1934.

From the artistic as well as the economic point of view, the unproduced plays represent a high element of risk. For there has been no way of being certain that the new plays could be acted. They are not written in the scorching prose of *Juno and the Paycock* and *The Plough and the Stars*. They illustrate a conscious, stubborn attempt to develop an artistic form that makes freer use of the theatre and reaches out toward universality of meaning.

For many years, Mr O'Casey has been living in Devonshire, England, not only in exile from Ireland, but in exile from the professional theatre. There has been no way of checking his imagination and eloquence against the capacities of the stage.

The profoundly moving performance of *Red Roses for Me*, as staged by John O'Shaughnessy, shows that Mr O'Casey has not been tilting at windmills. *Red Roses for Me* has greater stature and darker beauty on the stage than it had between the covers of a book.

In print it seems parochial and pedantic. But Mr O'Shaughnessy, who first directed it in Houston in 1951, has resolved the details of the story and the changes of mood into an ode of the valor of mankind — some of it funny, some of it sad and tragic, but all of it full of the compassion of an unconquerable writer who loves the human race with religious devotion. For the details of the play — the gusty, low comedy of the first two acts, the joyous dance of the third and the bitter tragedy of the last — are like movements in a symphony of mankind. Mr O'Shaughnessy knows that the real subject is the mind and soul of the author.

It is interesting to consider the development of Mr O'Casey as a writer since he left Ireland in a huff about twenty-five years ago. The story of *Red Roses for Me* is based on a Dublin railway strike in 1913–14 that provoked 'the bloody Easter Week Rising in

* *The New York Times* (8 Jan. 1956).

1916,' which, in turn, led to Irish national freedom. The Easter Rising is the setting for *The Plough and the Stars* and the prelude of *Juno and the Paycock*, which portrayed the Dublin of 1922. Mr O'Casey wrote both those plays at white heat, scornful of senseless slaughter and the muddle of Irish life. He wrote them naturalistically out of painful personal experience. No doubt they are the most enduring of the O'Casey plays. The feeling they express is highly concentrated.

By 1943, when he wrote *Red Roses for Me*, Mr O'Casey was still preoccupied with the experience that had scarred his soul when he was in his thirties. But in 1943 the direction of his writing was away from the particular to the general. Note how the dialogue keeps moving toward universal absolutes: 'I tell you,' Ayamonn says, 'life is not one thing but many things, a wide-branching flame, grand and good to see and feel, dazzling to the eye of no one loving it.'

It is a play of affirmation. In the affectionate relationship between Ayamonn and his gallant mother, there is a lot of autobiography. But the whole play may be regarded as spiritual autobiography. It expresses Mr O'Casey's delight in God and mankind. 'I tell you it is a gay sight for God to see joy shine for a moment on the faces of His much-troubled children,' Ayamonn exclaims.

Off stage and on the margins of *Red Roses of Me*, there is a lot of strife and violence. But it is a play that says yes to love, joy, courage and dreams of a better world. In 1943, in his early sixties, Mr O'Casey was far removed from the physical combat of his youth and was meditating on the eternal verities, all of which represent God to him.

To Mr O'Casey, the Orphic literary style comes naturally. Having educated himself on the Bible and Shakespeare, he cannot write a flat sentence. The dialogue of *Red Roses for Me* and the several songs strewn through it have melody and imagery beyond anything written for the stage today. But the richness of the literary style is no mannerism. The exuberance of living characters sweeps through it.

They are rugged individualists, reflecting Mr O'Casey in this respect, also. Nothing seems to make any impression on them. Although they wrangle with each other over religion, politics, and philosophy, they remain unregenerate each wedded imperishably to his own convictions, impervious to argument or reason. The nature of many of the arguments is petty or futile. But the flowing style gives them a comic eccentricity that is hilarious. And although the environment is generally squalid, Mr O'Casey's style of writing puts a little glory in it.

Like all O'Casey plays, *Red Roses for Me* is saturated in Irish life. It must have been difficult to assemble a cast that would be able to preserve the Irish flavor. Eileen Crowe, well remembered here from Abbey Theatre visitations, has come from Dublin to play the part of the mother. She is ideal, as everyone knew she would be. Her acting is sweet without being sentimental, and her musical speech is entrancing.

But the actors recruited from the United States are equally excellent: Kevin McCarthy as the young man ravenous for all the good things in life; Joyce Sullivan as the maiden troubled and bewildered by the young man's intransigence; E.G. Marshall as a garrulous buffoon; Ann Dere as a strong-minded tenement woman; Whitford Kane as a pious verger; Casey Walters as an insufferable atheist; and Eamon Flynn as a belligerent nationalist and Roman Catholic give lively performances in different keys, all of them Irish, all of them passionate and colorful.

And all of them full of the flaming spirit of Mr O'Casey. For they all represent his view of life, which is homely in environment but grand in speech and aspiration. He has caught it beautifully in the concluding song of the drama:

> A sober black shawl hides her body entirely.
> Thouch'd be th' sun an' the salt spray of th' sea;
> But down in th' darkness a slim hand, so lovely;
> Carries a rich bunch of red roses for me!

NOTES

1. For cast list and other production details, see pp. 91–3, Atkinson's column, 'Theatre: Sean O'Casey' (29 Dec. 1955).

Theatre: The O'Casey*

Although we had to wait sixteen years to see Sean O'Casey's *Purple Dust*, no hard feelings now. The performance that opened at Cherry Lane last evening is gusty and humorous.[1]

Thanks in part go to Philip Burton, who has staged it. For the delay in getting *Purple Dust* on the boards in New York is due largely to the fact that it is not an easy play to perform. It is a harum-scarum piece of low comedy and poetic rhapsody — two elements that do not usually associate on friendly terms. When some competent technicians tried to stage *Purple Dust* in London about three years ago, the dichotomy of the script defeated them.

But Mr Burton has overwhelmed the script with an exuberant performance that does not pretend to be logical or orderly. It is more like a gambol than a conventional play. Mr O'Casey's knock-about humors and his purple prose have been blended into a theatrical entertainment.

Purple Dust is the chronicle of two snobbish Britishers who try to cultivate the gracious life in an old mansion in Ireland. Having set up his victims, Mr O'Casey proceeds to knock them down with a slap-stick and a vocabulary.

For the self-conscious culture of two British nabobs who are worshipping the past is no match for the native cunning of Irish workmen, nor for the instincts of a couple of susceptible young ladies who love the romantic conversation of two Irish swains. Mr O'Casey means to say that worship of the past is arid, that urbane people are fools in the country, and that love is a closer bond between men and women than a good bank account. Like a loyal Irishman, he also reminds his British nabobs that Ireland had a golden culture when the English were savages.

Possibly he is trying to say too much; possibly he is trying to give too much philosophical depth to a comedy antic. If so, Mr Burton and the actors are not disconcerted. They carry it off with contagious enthusiasm. Lester Polakov has provided them with a set that makes the tiny stage at the Cherry Lane look about seven miles deep, and he has dressed them in something that approaches carnival attire. Everything has been arranged for a ludicrous rumpus.

* *The New York Times* (28 Dec. 1956).

That's the mood of the performance. After playing the parts of blameless gentlemen for years, Harry Bannister is immensely funny as one of O'Casey's end-men. His petulance and fatuousness as a misplaced London stockbroker are spontaneous and comic. The cast is in high spirits all the way through — Mary Welch and Kathleen Murray as the faithless young ladies; Paul Shyre as a querulous English pedant; P.J. Kelly as a guileful priest; Mike Kellin, Stephen Elliott, Robert Geiringer and Alvin Epstein as Irishmen with the gift of the gab. Mr Elliott deserves a special note of gratitude for the rapture with which he speaks a long, extravagantly figured speech in the midst of bedlam. Nothing could be less pertinent to that moment.

But Mr O'Casey is not an author who makes things easy for actors. By insisting on putting everything in the moment it occurs to him, he sets his actors problems. In their robustly amusing performance, the actors and their director have solved the problem with gusto. They have made *Purple Dust* an enjoyable frolic.

NOTES

1. New York premiere, Cherry Lane Theatre, 27 December 1956. This was the longest run for any O'Casey play — 14 months. Director, Philip Burton.

Cast:		
	First Workman	Mike Kellin
	Second Workman	Stephen Elliott
	Third Workman	Robert Geiringer
	Cyril Poges	Harry Bannister
	Souhaun	Mary Welch
	Barney	James Kenny
	Avril	Kathleen Murray
	Basil Stoke	Paul Shyre
	Cloyne	Betty Henritze
	O'Killigain	Alvin Epstein
	Yellow-Bearded Man	Sandy Kenyon
	Rev. George Canon Creehewel	P.J. Kelly
	Postmaster	Stefan Gierasch
	Figure	Alan Bermann
	Designed by	Lester Polakov

Comic Exuberance*

When Sean O'Casey wrote *Purple Dust* in 1940 Britain was fighting with her back to the wall. It seemed in doubtful taste to let an Irishman jeer at the British when the Germans were bombing them.

Since the war, *Purple Dust* has been repeatedly announced for production in New York and repeatedly put back on the shelf. Perhaps the fact that like Shaw, whom he revered, Mr O'Casey professes to be a Communist has congealed the pocket-books of backers. Mr O'Casey is a turrible man on paper. At home with his family and friends he is a mild and lovable old codger disarmingly humble about his talent. But put a piece of paper in front of him and he starts hurling thunder-bolts over the landscape. He has more feuds up his sweater sleeve than the Hatfields and McCoys. 'The Green Crow,' as he calls himself in his last book,[1] is a turrible cawer.

By paying no attention to his peripheral wrangles, four producing partners have now succeeded in getting *Purple Dust* on the stage of the Cherry Lane where it is likely to have a good engagement.[2] It has been directed by Philip Burton, who has not been discouraged by Mr O'Casey's vagrant craftsmanship. And it is acted by a troupe of good-humored actors who speak the works as they were written and do not try to psychoanalyze the parts. Taken at face value *Purple Dust* turns out to be an amusing row-de-dow that mixes philosophy with horseplay.

Literally, it is the story of a rich English stockbroker and a supercilious English pedant who try to renovate a beautiful Tudor house in Ireland and live elegantly in bucolic surroundings. But they are frustrated by the Irish workmen, who are not the least impressed by English wealth and culture, and who have a ruinously heavy hand with rare furniture and household treasures. Two of the Irishmen also charm away the two Irish girls who have come over from England as mistresses of the middle-aged patrons of art.

Although Mr O'Casey has denied that these two snobs represent England to him, they certainly represent a form of British gentility that he despises. And some of the things his Irish characters

* *The New York Times* (6 Jan. 1957).

say are not likely to win the devotion of the English among whom he has lived for a quarter of a century. 'In a generation or so the English Empire will be remembered only as a half-forgotten nursery rhyme,' says O'Killigain.

Purple Dust is not one of Mr O'Casey's epic dramas. It is a rough-and-ready comedy that illustrates the author's basic convictions: that life should be lived joyously by everyone; that freedom includes not only free speech, but freedom from cant, freedom from stuffy conventions, freedom from social humbug of all kinds. As usual, the literary style is both comic and rhapsodic. The lowliest Irish workmen speak in glorious rhythms.

Apart from the production of *Red Roses for Me*, which was the victim of a booking tangle last year, none of Mr O'Casey's new plays has been done in New York since 1934. On local stages he has been represented by several revivals and the two excellent reading performances made from two volumes of his autobiography — *I Knock at the Door* and *Pictures in the Hallway*.[3]

Purple Dust, wayward in form as well as content, brings us his humor, eloquence and humanity in a robust performance at a cozy theatre. Although the Irish accents got up for the occasion by local players are not ravishing, the actors, the director and the costume and scene designer are bringing us some of the O'Casey gusto, which is wholesome, tonic and entertaining.

NOTES

1. *The Green Crow* (1956), a collection of essays.
2. For cast details see pp. 97–8, Atkinson's column, 'Theatre: The O'Casey' (28 Dec. 1956).
3. See footnote 4 p. 108, in Atkinson's column, 'Two by O'Casey' (23 Nov. 1958).

O'Casey's Defense of Joy*

'COCK-A-DOODLE DANDY HAS PREMIERE HERE'

After crowing in other parts of North America, Sean O'Casey's *Cock-a-Doodle Dandy* flapped its wings and crowed last evening at the Carnegie Hall Playhouse.[1]

This is the fantastic morality play that Mr O'Casey wrote a decade ago in defense of joy and in condemnation of meanness. In philosophy and in the freedom of its craftsmanship, it is the grandest play of his post-war period.

Since it was written on the amiable assumption that all actors are as pungent as Barry Fitzgerald and F.J. McCormick, it also sets the theatre serious problems. The current performance improves as the play advances and ends beautifully and dramatically. But not all the problems have been solved in the first act and part of the second.

The cock is Mr O'Casey's symbol of joy. In general the play records the ageless struggle between those who take delight in being alive and those who represent suspicion, fear and intolerance. Years ago Mr O'Casey gave up writing realistic plays, assuming no doubt that he has as much right to freedom of expression as the happy characters in his plays.

Cock-a-Doodle Dandy is, therefore, an imaginative fantasy in which the cock crows and leaps about the landscape, evil spirits put a curse on a bottle of whisky, eerie voices terrify the joyless people and banshees explode inside the house. There are also songs and dances, a few turns of horseplay and one or two ceremonial scenes. Mr O'Casey is not a prudent workman.

In the theatre, *Cock-a-Doodle Dandy* has to be played like a dance — all lightness and improvisation, bursting with spontaneity. The early sequences in the current production do not have that much cohesion and grace. As the scene designer, Lester Polakov has managed to catch the elemental unreality of an Irish house and garden; the scenery and the lighting are excellent. So is the exuberant cock, sardonically costumed by Don Jansen, acted with amusing bravado by Carlo Mazzone.

But the play as a whole refuses to take wing in these introduc-

* *The New York Times* (13 Nov. 1958).

tory sequences because Will Geer and Ian Martin, the Captain Boyle and the Joxer of *Cock-a-Doodle Dandy*, are not Irish. It is not a matter of accent chiefly. It is a matter of characterization. Mr Geer and Mr Martin, good actors on more sensible occasions, cannot communicate the tight-jawed fanaticism of hot-tempered hypocrites who are intoxicated with the sound of words they do not understand and advertise their ignorance with literary bravado. They are closer to Mutt and Jeff than to Boyle and Joxer.

The Celtic tone is uneven throughout the cast. Probably there is nothing that Philip Burton, the director, can do about that. And some of his actors are first-rate, Irish or not: Paul Shyre as an addle-headed soothsayer and moralist; George Ebeling as a harsh, bellowing priest; Anne Meara as a giggling, high-spirited servant; Rae Allen as a fiery-eyed young wife to an old codger; Gaby Rodgers as a shameless hussy; Jack Betts as a mysterious messenger who is not intimidated by superstition or authority; John Aronson as a terrified police sergeant.

When the theme begins to emerge from the harum-scarum narrative mid-way of the second act, the acting does convey Mr O'Casey's vigorous personality. An Irish prophet, undismayed by the post-war world, he punishes the hypocrites and takes to the high road in the company of the fearless people, leaving the rubble of the garden with a lyrical song.

The last act is particularly well written, for it is decisive and merciful. Fortunately, the acting is at its best in these somber, climactical moments: Mr Geer disconsolate before the door of his empty house, the girls on their way to some happier region, the mysterious messenger singing a farewell song.

Cock-a-Doodle Dandy is a grand play. Although the current performance is imperfect, it accomplishes one excellent thing: it has got the text out of the book and on to a stage.

NOTES

1. New York premiere, Carnegie Hall Playhouse, 12 November 1958. Director, Philip Burton.

Cast:	*The Cock*	Carlo Mazzone
	Michael Marthraun	Will Geer
	Sailor Mahan	Ian Martin
	Lorna	Rae Allen

Loreleen	Gaby Rodgers
Marion	Anne Meara
Shanaar	Paul Shyre
First Rough Fellow	Dennis Drew
Second Rough Fellow	David Faulkner
Father Domineer	George Ebeling
The Sergeant	John Aronson
Jack (The Lorry Driver)	Paul Hinxmann
Julia	Carroll Conroy
One-Eyed Larry	Frank Groseclose
The Messenger	Jack Betts
A Porter	M. David Samples
A Mayor	Sidney Kay
A Macebearer	Howard Lee
Julia's Father	M. David Samples
The Bellman	Sidney Kay
A Nun	Ailsa Dawson
Designed by	Lester Polakov

Theatre: A Prologue to Greatness*

SHADOW OF A GUNMAN BY O'CASEY AT BIJOU

Thanks to the Actors Studio, Sean O'Casey's *Shadow of a Gunman* has fallen heir to a masterly performance, which was put on at the Bijou last evening.[1] The play is all alive; every part is brilliantly acted.

Although the Abbey troupe included *Shadow of a Gunman* in its repertory here in 1932,[2] most New York theatregoers have never seen it. Written in 1923, it is the first full-length play by O'Casey that reached the stage.

Juno and the Paycock and *The Plough and the Stars* are more powerful and passionate. But *Shadow of a Gunman,* written in the same idiom, is a fascinating prologue to greatness, full of the same ironic humor, sharpened with the same tragic irony at the end.

Set in a squalid tenement in Dublin in 1920, it portrays the life

* *The New York Times* (21 Nov. 1958).

of some obscure Irish people during the time of the bloody
rebellion. Until the end, nothing happens in the usual sense of a
dramatic story. But Mr O'Casey's sketches of a handful of shiftless
Irish people have more vitality than more stage narratives; and
the raffish dialogue with its querulous mannerisms and its learned
allusions is illuminating and comic and original. Mr O'Casey
wrote it out of his own experience; and it has the spontaneity of
truth.

As in the two following plays, *Shadow of a Gunman* changes
from comedy to tragedy without warning and wipes the smile off
a theatregoer's face before he knows what has happened. Two
aimless, futile Irish young men let a romantic girl upstairs take
responsibility for some bombs that have been left in their room.
They never raise a finger to help her when the British tommies
hustle her off to their lorry. She dies in an ambush while they
quiver in their boots at home. By this savage twist in the concluding scene Mr O'Casey expresses his contempt for the stupid
level on which rebellion is conducted under the panoply of brave
songs and boastful phrases.

Granted that the play is a piece of extraordinary stage literature, the Actors Studio players under the direction of Jack
Garfein are entitled to equal recognition. Seldom is a script
brought to such vivid life. To put the performance in proper perspective, one thinks of the Moscow Art Theatre's *The Lower
Depths* as something comparable in style and viewpoint. Peter
Larkin's setting of a rag-tag, cluttered tenement room; Tharon
Musser's pulsing light-plot, and Ruth Morley's messy costumes
give the play visual vitality.

There is nothing makeshift about any of the characterizations.
The people of the play are sharply individualized in a whole range
of tones from the bravado of William Smithers' egotistical poet to
the willowy freshness of Susan Strasberg's starry-eyed girl, the
timid pedantry of Arthur Malet's scribe, and the flamboyance of
George Mathews' tipsy roister.

If no one is starred, the point is well taken. For it would be
difficult to argue that any one contributes more to the turbulence
of the performance than the others. Gerald O'Loughlin's cautious
peddler of trifles, Zamah Cunningham's overbearing, self-
righteous biddy, Katherine Squire's colorless wife to a bully,
Daniel Reed's peevish landlord, Bruce Dern's nervous, laconical
rebel, Stefan Gierasch's swaggering neighbor, James Greene's

pitiless tommy are all clearly drawn character portraits.

It seems to this theatregoer that the pace of the first act is too torpid for a play about such quicksilver people. But that may be intended as contrast with the tension of the second act. For Mr Garfein seems to be a director who likes to construct scenes that vary the pitch of the drama. They are excellent. The details are as carefully executed as the structure of the performance as a whole.

The performance meets the play on equal terms. And *Shadow of a Gunman* is literature that gives an impression of being unpremeditated, not so much like something written as something that simply is.

NOTES

1. Revived by Cheryl Crawford and Joel Schenker by arrangement with the Actors' Studio, Inc., at the Bijou Theatre, 20 November 1958. Total performances: 52

Cast:		
	Donal Davoren	William Smithers
	Seumas Shields	Gerald O'Loughlin
	Maguire	Bruce Dern
	Mr Mulligan	Daniel Reed
	Minnie Powell	Susan Strasberg
	Tommy Owens	Stefan Gierasch
	Mrs Henderson	Zamah Cunningham
	Mr Gallogher	Arthur Malet
	Mrs Grigson	Katherine Squire
	Adolphus Grigson	George Mathews
	Auxiliary	James Greene
	Passers-by	Jack Allen
		Tammy Allen
		Hilda Brawner
		Tom Wheatley

Staged by Jack Garfein
Settings by Peter Larkin
Lighting by Tharon Musser
Costumes by Ruth Morley

Two by O'Casey*

COCK-A-DOODLE DANDY AND SHADOW OF A GUNMAN OPEN WITHIN 9 DAYS

Within a space of nine days New York has had an opportunity to see one of Sean O'Casey's earliest plays and one of his latest. *Shadow of a Gunman* (1923), which was put on last Thursday, is the first O'Casey play acted by Dublin's Abbey Theatre.[1] *Cock-a-Doodle Dandy*, which opened Nov. 12, represents the epic style in which he was writing in 1949.[2]

When he wrote *Shadow of a Gunman* he had a specific topic — the 'throubles' in Dublin — and he had in mind a specific company of actors. His two most memorable plays, *Juno and the Paycock* and *The Plough and the Stars*, appeared in the next three years and represent a refinement of *Shadow of a Gunman* method. Since these plays are vigorous and pungent, full of caustic humor and bitter recriminations, and since they can be acted idiomatically, many people regard them as Mr O'Casey's greatest achievements and his later plays as pretentious rhetoric.

There is no doubt that his first three plays are among the best written in this century. The violent contrasts of humor and tragedy, the racy characterizations, the anger, the fundamental humanity of their viewpoint compose magnificent dramas written at white heat. In our day the theatre's most memorable cry of agony is Juno Boyle's penultimate speech in *The Paycock*: 'Sacred heart o' Jesus, take away our hearts o' stone, and give us hearts o' flesh! Take away this murdherin' hate, an' give us Thine own eternal love!'

Since the scheduled opening of *Shadow of a Gunman* was postponed one day last week, it is not possible to discuss the performance in today's article.

Even if Mr O'Casey were susceptible to other people's opinions, it would be futile to expect him to go on repeating himself throughout his career. There is no surer way of boring the public. Every since he wrote *The Silver Tassie* in 1928, Mr O'Casey has been writing plays in a more improvised form that encompass wider territory and portray Mankind instead of individual men.

---

* *The New York Times* (23 Nov. 1958).

Cock-a-Doodle Dandy is the one he regards as his best. Although it is founded on two garrulous, pig-headed Irishmen who are as realistic as Captain Boyle and Joxer, it is a comic fantasy full of sprites and hobgoblins, supernatural hocus-pocus, dances and songs and bits of religious ceremony. It says 'yes' to the people young enough in heart to enjoy the sensation of being alive, and it shows the mournful consequences of attempts to deny life through greed, prejudice, dogma and fear. (The last word in the last volume of Mr O'Casey's autobiography[3] is 'Hurrah!')

Cock-a-Doodle Dandy has been available in book form (Macmillan) for several years. But there is still no certainty that it can be acted. The current performance does not draw the humorous exaltation out of it. Until the story settles down in the last act to the rueful consequences of meanness and intolerance, the performance does not preserve the astringent vitality of Mr O'Casey's writing.

These comments are set down here with some reluctance because the job of getting a professional performance of the play on the stage represents a labor of love in which the labor has been excessive. Having put on the two O'Casey's readings and *Purple Dust*,[4] Paul Shyre has now undertaken a more difficult play that has defeated several other theatre people who have tried to organize a production. The fairy-story set by Lester Polakov creates the proper mood, and most of the supernatural strokes are plausibly represented.

It is pleasant to add that Mr Shyre turns out to be the drollest actor in the company. As the doddering, itinerant evangelist, he captures the foolish pedantry of the part in a vein of humor that preserves the O'Casey irony and gleam. The contrast between the grand manner of the character and the woolly dialogue is both satirical and realistic.

Without humorous acting in the parts of the two chief numbskulls, it is impossible to catch the mischievous gaiety of the play as a whole. Will Geer and Ian Martin are miscast in these two roles. They are too slow and too literal. Read their first-act dialogue: it bubbles over with the comic guile, bogus eloquence and hard-headed ignorance characteristic of other O'Casey characters. Although the writing is richly figured, it is always brisk, succinct and spontaneous; it ought to be as funny as Dogberry. But Mr Geer and Mr Martin have a ponderous touch; there is no electricity in what they do. Although Philip Burton, the director, has staged the sober conclusion of the play impressively, he has not been able to set free the high spirits of the first half.

When Mr O'Casey wrote *Cock-a-Doodle Dandy* he had been living apart from the theatre for years. No doubt the actors he had in the back of his head were the Abbey Theatre troupe that reared him in the Twenties. Even if that company still existed, it is doubtful that they could act a play written in such a freehand style. They were essentially realistic in method. *Juno and the Paycock* and *The Plough and the Stars* fitted them perfectly.

But *Cock-a-Doodle Dandy* is more like *Peer Gynt* or a ballet with spoken dialogue or a piece of music like *Till Eulenspiegel*. Unless a company can play it in balanced tones and rhythms it comes close to being 'one hell of a disorder,' as one of the characters remarks. Mr O'Casey, who will be 79 in March, was seventy when he wrote this last of his comic reveries. It is like a testament of faith in the delight of life. The man who wrote *Shadow of a Gunman* in the fury of his youth wrote *Cock-a-Doodle Dandy* in the serenity of old age. It is the same man — the dedication still high, the heat cooled a good deal by humor and experience.

NOTES

1. Bijou Theatre, 20 November 1958. Total performances: 52. Director, Jack Garfein.
2. See pp. 101–3, Atkinson's column, 'O'Casey's Defense of Joy' (13 Nov. 1958).
3. *Sunset and Evening Star* (1954).
4. Shyre adapted *Pictures in the Hallway* in 1956. Staged at the Playhouse, New York, 16 September 1956. Total performances: 19. Director, Stuart Vaughan. In 1957 Shyre adapted *I Knock at the Door*. Staged at the Belasco Theatre, New York, 29 September 1957. Total performances: 48. Director, Stuart Vaughan. For Shyre's production of *Purple Dust*, see pp. 97–8, Atkinson's column, 'Theatre: The O'Casey (28 Dec. 1956).

Theatre: *Triple Play**

If you add the Chekhov sketch, *Triple Play*, which opened at the Playhouse last evening.[1] consists of four items. They are all acting

* *The New York Times* (16 Apr. 1959).

pieces for Jessica Tandy and Hume Cronyn, troupers in good form and good standing. ... In the two O'Casey comedies, they overburden the fun with acting.

A Pound on Demand is a brawl concerned with a drunken man in a post office in Dublin. He is trying to draw £1 out of his post office savings account. Since the sketch is a thin one, it probably needs a fat performance. Miss Tandy, Mr Cronyn, Biff McGuire, George Mathews and Margot Stevenson go at it with all the gags in an actor's notebook.

Bedtime Story is a shrewder comedy. It is the story of a hypocritical Dublin bachelor who is trying to evict a hussy from his room at 4 in the morning without alerting his landlady. Mr Cronyn and Miss Tandy play it with the wild abandon of a farce — always in motion and always at the top of their voices.

But there is more than a low-comedy romp in *Bedtime Story*. Beneath the surface fun, it satirizes the timidity and respectability of the perfect hypocrite. It expresses the O'Casey contempt for the pious charlatan. By playing it all in one key and one tempo, Miss Tandy and Mr Cronyn miss the most genuine part of the comedy, which is the satire of character in the midst of a tense situation.

The settings for *Triple Play* are by David Hays and the costumes by Anna Hill Johnstone. They represent the high standards that prevail through the whole production.

Although *Triple Play* is designed for a holiday for audiences as well as a pair of well-loved actors, it seems to this theatregoer to be best when the mood is serious. Miss Tandy's soft portrait of an unloved lady, lost in rueful dreams, Mr Cronyn's humorous portrait of an unloved man broken in spirit — are the most memorable items in this bill of theatre miniatures.

NOTES

1. Four one-act plays (*Portrait of a Madonna*, by Tennessee Williams; *The Harmful Effects of Tobacco*, by Anton Chekhov; and *A Pound on Demand* and *Bedtime Story* by Sean O'Casey) presented by the Theatre Guild and Dore Schary at the Playhouse Theatre, 15 April 1959. Only the criticism of the O'Casey plays is given here.

Cast:	*A Pound on Demand*	
Girl in Charge		Margot Stevenson
Jerry		Hume Cronyn
Sammy		Biff McGuire
The Public		Jessica Tandy
Policeman		George Mathews

Bedtime Story

John Jo Mulligan	Hume Cronyn
Angela Nightingale	Jessica Tandy
Daniel Halibut	Biff McGuire

BOTH PLAYS: Staged by Hume Cronyn
Setting and lighting by David Hays
Costumes by Anna Hill Johnston

*Triple Play**

BILL OF MINIATURES BY THREE DRAMATISTS

Since the theatre tries to survive at the box office by devastating
the customers, there is seldom any room for modest bits and
pieces.

In *Triple Play*, Jessica Tandy and Hume Cronyn have violated
show business rules by assembling an evening of short plays and a
monologue: . . .[1]

Both as director and actor, Mr Cronyn interprets the two
O'Casey vaudevilles as slam-bang farce. This is a sensible approach to *A Pound on Demand*, which is a labored jest about two
rowdy Irishmen baffled by the bureaucratic decorum of a Dublin
post office.

But the slam-bang style blunts a good deal of the entertainment concealed in *Bedtime Story*. In this one-act piece a timid
young Irish prig with a wanton lady in his furnished room at 3:15
A.M., Mr O'Casey is not an empty laugher. In addition to having
a good time he is satirizing prudishness and hypocrisy.

Bedtime Story has been acted at Arena Stage in Washington
and at the Alley Theatre in Houston, Texas, and probably in
other places as well. In Washington and Houston the acting style
was more varied and subtle. Expressed in a lower key, it drew
sardonic contrast between the amorousness of the occasion and
the remorse and terror of the young man. Since he is alarmed by
the possibility that his landlady will hear a woman's voice in his

* *The New York Times* (26 Apr. 1959).

rented room, the controlled volume of the performance accented the stealthiness of the situation; there was a sense of pressure from the outside.

In Mr Cronyn's staging, the performance is egghead low comedy. It puts the emphasis on the broad and raucous style of the acting rather than the shrewd humors of the play. Although Miss Tandy and Mr Cronyn are versatile actors, they are best when their craftmanship is subtle. Tennessee Williams and Chekhov are their most becoming authors in their evening of informal entertainment.

NOTES

1. For production details see pp. 108–10, Atkinson's article, 'Theatre: Triple Play' (16 Apr. 1959). Only the criticism of the O'Casey plays is given here.

Newly Published Plays*

Ah, my heart is weary all alone
And it sends a lonely cry
To the land that sings beyond my dreams
And the lonely Sundays pass by.
Ah, the quiet land of Erin.
                    — O'Casey

What doth the Green Crow say? He says that young people should take pagan delight in the pleasures of love.

The Green Crow, as he calls himself, is Sean O'Casey, 81 years old, who has just published three short plays that have not yet been produced (Macmillan, London). In self-imposed exile from Ireland, which he left more than thirty years ago, he sits in Torquay, Devon, brooding on the misfortunes of his native land. Since an inflammation in his eyes requires treatment every three hours and respiratory ailments frequently afflict him, it is diffi-

* *The New York Times* (14 July 1961).

cult to know whence he summons the strength to go on writing plays.

Despite the infirmities the second of the three plays, *Figuro in the Night*, is a gay and mocking improvisation that retains the freshness of his spirit and style. Taking as his theme, 'The Ferocious Chastity of Ireland,' he hurls another thunderbolt at the censoriousness of the Roman Catholic Church in Ireland, with which he has been skirmishing for years.

Figuro in the Night begins with a sad conversation between an old man and old woman who have gone through life without love. Having been convinced in their youth that love was a sin, they have made a vocation of pious chastity. 'I turned away from petticoat an' bodice, an' banished myself brightly under a Bishop's blessing,' says the old man proudly. Although the old woman has a few vagrant regrets, she also is proud of her lifetime of denial. Crotchety and wizened, they discuss love as if it were something unholy and unclean.

But then 'the cawing of a crow comes down clean from the sky' and disturbs the complacence of the old bachelor and spinster. Obviously, the crow is green. He has a mischievous influence on Dublin as well as the play, and the young people rush together in a joyous dance.

Mr O'Casey, who is as contrary as any of his characters, has introduced here some Priapean rites that will make it difficult to produce *Figuro in the Night* in Ireland, or on Broadway, for that matter. For Mr O'Casey abhors either prudery or prudence. Having taken a good theme, however, and having found the right form in which to develop it, he has made *Figuro in the Night* into a sunny play — the style sweet and humorous without being florid. In the concluding scene, the young maiden at the window sings to her swain one of Mr O'Casey's traditional verses:

> You've brought me th' bonnie blue ribbon,
> So lovely, so rich an' so fair;
> So I'll open the door, an' then dare you
> To tie up my bonnie brown hair.

The new volume also includes a capital one-act farce called *The Moon Shines on Kylenamoe* — an affectionate cartoon of the Irish country temperament when it is provoked by a aloof Englishman. The third play, *Behind the Green Curtains*, is a propaganda play. Having been jilted by a capitalist, the brave heroine transfers her passion to a Communist with an alacrity that destroys everything in the play except the message.

For the Green Crow, always embattled, is not giving an inch on any quarter. Wherever he sees a head, he pecks it. The pecking in *Figuro in the Night* is whimsically good-natured. Out of humor, wisdom and audacity Mr O'Casey has composed one of his gayest pleasantries. His heart is now weary, and his writing hand is sure.

Part III
The Autobiographies

Insurgent Penman*

SEAN O'CASEY'S AUTOBIOGRAPHY

While this department was gloomily pondering these notions,[1] the postman knocked twice and brought in a copy of Sean O'Casey's *I Knock at the Door*, a book of autobiographical impressions of his first twelve years in Dublin. Macmillan has published it in London and will publish it in New York some time next Summer. According to gossip around town, in a play he has also just finished,[2] Mr O'Casey turns out to be a revolutionary incarnadined; he paints the star of Bethlehem red. If so, no one will accuse the caustic Irishman of dabbling in the revolution. For he has come out of the lower depths of the pain and poverty and the sodden grime of common labor, and the first thing to be considered in anything he writes is that he means every word of it, and the back of his hand to you, my boyo, if you are suspicious of his sincerity. Although Mr O'Casey has the soul of a religious poet, he has the hardness of a man who has worked with his hands and raised his croaking voice in song in the Dublin pubs. Now he lives in the English countryside, where the airs are sweet and healing, but he has seen some terrible urban brawls in his time; at the age of 54 he can still brawl in print with the most vituperative. His ideas come out of harsh, grinding experience.

If Mr Auden and Mr Isherwood seem to this department to be posturing the revolution in their precociously written stage plays, Mr O'Casey now and then postures art in *I Knock at the Door*. When he is writing realistically, his style is biting and vivid — blunt words, short sentences, direct hits every time. But as if those were not characteristics of a great writer, he frequently indulges himself in pages of Joycean soliloquy in the stream-of-consciousness method. The central character of this autobiography is a lad of the tenderest years, but the spectacle of a neighborhood

* *The New York Times* (9 Apr. 1939).

ster mourning beside his father's coffin provokes him into a
long sequence of mature thoughts, some of them obscene, that
flow like shadows through his mind, and the spectacle of the
parson solemnly officiating at the grave starts another unreadable
eruption of words. Mr O'Casey also vexes his pages with dream
fantasies that are pretty hard to take at one sitting. There is a
word for this sort of imitative writing; it is 'punk.' Every man kills
the thing he loves; and Mr O'Casey, who can write dialogue like a
man inspired, can supernaturalize like an amateur poseur.[3]

Fortunately, these pages of brummagem are merely intrusions
upon a book that is otherwise worthy of the author. For Mr
O'Casey has a keen mind, incandescent emotions and a muscular
writing hand, and the pinched life he led as a boy in Dublin yields
the finest story he has put between covers. His father died when
he was too young to understand much of anything, his mother
had a desperately hard time in keeping her youngest child and
herself warm and nourished, and the boy was afflicted with
agonizing eye trouble most of his youth. Mr O'Casey does not
dramatize it or draw a moral from it. To the artist in him it is
merely evidence of life. Most of it he sets down impersonally, with
a kind of joy in the vividness of his memories.

No one but a man hardened by the most elementary experience
could write so trenchantly the story of going to Sunday School on
a rainy day, of the fight in an alley after day school, of the
inhuman aggressiveness of the parson, of the mournful Jew
taunted by Irish urchins, of the eye treatments in a hospital, of
the cow who separated from the drover's herd and sat down
wearily in the middle of the sidewalk and stayed there far into the
night, of the games in the street and the first love affair. It was a
Dublin of fierce religious partisanship — intolerantly Catholic or
Protestant. The Parnell cleavage was equally bitter. *I Knock at
the Door* is an illuminating book by one of the most genuine
dramatists of today, and when it is not artistically self-conscious,
it is the pure art of a man of strength, courage and honesty. If he
wants to be a revolutionary he is entitled to lay about him with a
pen dipped in the red ink bottle.

NOTES

1. The original title of this article was 'Insurgent Penmen.' The first half dealt
   with W.H. Auden and Christopher Isherwood.

2. *The Stars Turns Red*, published in 1940.

3. O'Casey responded to this review. In a letter dated only 'April 1939' he wrote to Atkinson:

> I do get tremendous joy out of the writing of fantasy, more than out of any-
> thing else... And of another thing, dear Brooks, I am as positive as a
> human can be: there is no posing in the book from one end to the other —
> that is 'art' posing. For I can honestly say I don't care a tinker's damn
> about art, simply because I know nothing about it. But I love the way I
> imagine the Greeks wrote (from English translations) & I love the way I
> know the Elizabethans wrote; & I am anxious & eager to try to make use of
> both in the things I try to write. Ambitious? Damnably so; but, even so,
> what is success (if I succeed) or what is failure? (if I fail). Who can tell?

O'Casey Keeps his Life Moving*

Among the things for which one is permitted to be grateful just now is the publication of the second volume of Sean O'Casey's autobiography. The first volume, *I Knock at the Door*, appeared three years ago. The second volume is entitled *Pictures in the Hallway*, and carries the story of his career through adolescence into the early years of mature life. Since Mr O'Casey writes singing prose and has a native gift for dramatic portraiture, the appearance of the second volume of his vibrant chronicle of life in Dublin ought to be a welcome incident for readers in general.

But it is something of an event for writers. Mr O'Casey is a good man from whom to learn something about the relation of a writer to his work. To him, writing is not an end in itself but life transmuted into radiance. Although *Pictures in the Hallway* is autobiography you will find in it very little about Mr O'Casey's personal attributes. He is not interested in superficial things. Out of the bitterness of his experience he has written the drama of a boy tossed about in the shrill, mean chaos of city life, snatching

* *The New York Times* (5 Apr. 1942).

fragments of beauty out of turmoil and cupidity.

Mr O'Casey is a man of fierce pride. Bristling with antagonisms, he is a hard man in a fight. But *Pictures in the Hallway* is a modest book, for he is interested in himself only as one fiery particle in the vast firmament of human society. Many writers are more successful than Mr O'Casey. They have more readers, make more money and have wider influence. But Mr O'Casey is perfectly oriented in the universe. He has solved the writer's private problem. He is a free man and he does not need to bluff, pose or truckle.

There are many ways of living, and every writer has to solve his own problem according to his individuality and circumstances. But since we are discussing Mr O'Casey, let us consider how it comes about that he is so well adjusted to fundamental things. In the first place, he was born of good parents — a father of intelligence and spirit, a mother of humor and tenacity. Although the father died when Sean was young and left the family in poverty, he set the stamp that distinguished the O'Caseys from the ignorant poor. In the second place, the crushing poverty in which Sean lived for the first thirty-five or forty years of his life taught him the grim essentials of life and gave him a point of view.

Mr O'Casey does not wear his poverty on his sleeve. He asks for no pity on that score. Nor is he elated to have pulled out of it, for this is in no wise a success story. Poverty was merely the realistic truth of most of Dublin in those years. And it was real poverty — no overcoat, no blankets, no carfare, no money for doctors; and so meager were the wages when Sean had a job that the poverty could only be borne with stealing. Since it did not destroy his inner vitality, as it probably did in thousands of other cases, it taught him the basic necessities of life; and since he knew what he could live without, it strengthened his natural fearlessness. He had nothing to lose but his self-respect, which became priceless. Poverty developed in him a scorn for genteel respectability and a hatred of smugness, opportunism and avarice.

When he writes about the seamy side of life Mr O'Casey is, therefore, no amateur. There was plenty of filth in it, but he does not gloat over it or shock the reader with foul smells and obscenities. One of his chapters is devoted to the dung dodgers who came at intervals in the Dublin of no plumbing 'to empty out the potties and ashpits in the backyards of people, filling the whole place with a stench that didn't disappear for a week.' A braggart writer in the naturalistic vein would make something sensational of a noisome topic like that. But Mr O'Casey presents it as a common fact of life. He leaves you merely with the impression of how it degraded the people who had to cope with it.

No one can learn anything from books who has not first learned something basic about life. Mr O'Casey understands the function of books. Somewhere in *Pictures in the Hallway* he says of Johnny Casside (who is himself): 'From life he had learned much; and from books he would learn more of the wisdom thought out, and the loveliness imagined, by the wiser and greater brethren of the human family.'

Although Mr O'Casey's experience has put iron in his character and rubbed bitterness into his bones, he is also a man who loves songs and is exalted by beauty. None of the grinding drudgery of the world can dull his spirit. There is one good illustration of that. After pushing a rickety handcart piled with newspapers one day through the clattering traffic of the Dublin streets, Johnny Casside rattled down by the quays at sundown, and saw how the waning light ennobled the puddles, the grime and the dingy buildings. Everything was transfigured by the sunset and it make him glad:

> He shoved his handcart along again under the motley dome of the sky, tired, but joyous, praising God for His brightness and the will towards joy in the breasts of men, the swiftness of leg and foot in the heart of a dance, for the gift of song and laughter, for the sense of victory and the dream that God's right hand held firm.

Since 1924, when he was 40 years of age, Mr O'Casey has been a professional writer. He has written three or four of the finest plays in modern English. They are evidence of living. They come out of what he knows and is. In experience and understanding he is what a writer ought to be — honest and courageous in the sight of God.

O'Casey's Own Story*

IDERATION OF THE LATEST VOLUME IN THE AUTHOR'S AUTOBIOGRAPHY

During this interlude at the opening of a lazy season, it may be permissible to say something in praise of O'Casey's remarkable autobiography. It began in 1939 with *I Knock at the Door*, one of the most inspired books ever written about childhood. In 1942 came the second volume, *Pictures in the Hallway*, which carried the glorious record of a grubby career through boyhood and early youth. The current volume, *Drums under the Windows*, and incidentally the least exhilarating of the lot, takes Johnny Casside, or Sean O'Casey, through the wild and harebrained Irish Rebellion and the early years of World War I.

Here and there the extraordinary significance of this glowing autobiography has been appreciatively recognized by people who love men and literature. But there seems to be no general excitement about it. People are not expiring left and right with the usual apoplexy. Is a work of first quality so common that we accept it with casual enjoyment? As for myself, I am impatient at the prospect of having to wait another two years before the appearance of the fourth volume when, presumably, Mr O'Casey will get round to the time when he was writing *Juno and the Paycock*, *The Plough and the Stars* and *Shadow of a Gunman* for the Abbey Theatre. Waiting for the fourth volume is something worth living for — and that remark is not tossed in here lightly.

Since *Drums under the Windows* has less sustained magic than the two preceding volumes, this is not the best time to be sounding the brass in honor of the whole work. In the current volume Mr O'Casey is thrusting his sharp nose and chin into politics, which is man's unworthiest subject — particularly in Dublin where every man is his own politician and knows only what he is against. In the newest volume Mr O'Casey also indulges himself more than usual in long, loose, half-mystic flights of fancy designed for his private amusement. He is trying to adumbrate something there, but what it is only the good Lord knows, for it is gibberish in comparison with the sinewy prose he writes when he

* *The New York Times* (22 Sept. 1946).

has a concrete subject. Apart from these willful flights into the void, he is writing the best English prose of today. The works are plain enough. But the writing as a whole has great imaginative vitality, as though this autobiography were part novel, part poem and part lampoon of the universe. It is a fully orchestrated work of art with the core of a strong theme and many variations. Mr O'Casey is a virtuoso performer with pen and paper. But in the next volume, 'Come, leave this fancy way,' Johnny Casside, and stick to what you did, saw, thought and felt.

There are problems for the literary scholars; and this column must make an honest attempt to remain on its own side of the fence. Let us look at the record to discover what Mr O'Casey in the course of sixty-two years has brought to the stage and to this crowning autobiography. Compare him with Shaw and O'Neill, and it is obvious that his life's work is not voluminous. Everyone recognizes the genius of *Juno and the Paycock* and *The Plough and the Stars*. Fewer recognize the genius of *Within the Gates*, which is O'Casey's masque expressing faith in the world's dispossessed, written before the dispossessed became so appallingly numerous. Unless the future is a good deal richer than at the moment it promises to be, and unless it is overflowing with genius, these plays ought to be recognized as classics for a good many years. Even including three or four minor plays, like *Nannie's Night Out* (what could that have been like!) and later scripts that no one has been willing to produce, that is not a very obese record. What has O'Casey been up to all these years?

His autobiography gives the answer. Mr O'Casey has been living. And the plays he began to write in his forties were the products of hard and passionate living in the thick of the world's turmoil and suffering. The professional playwright lives in the world of the theatre. Having learned the technique of playmaking, he shops around for a suitable subject; and some excellent plays are joined in that fashion. But in Mr O'Casey's career, the writing of a few dramas has been incidental to living in a world of ordinary men and women who have worked for their bread and butter by the sweat of their brows.

Reared in poverty and tied to poverty by a thousand invisible threads that would not let him free, no wonder Mr O'Casey was, and perhaps still is, attracted by the idea of communism.

The wonder is that through the long, scouring years in the slums he kept in his soul some images of magnificence, as one of his countrymen phrased it. His brother sickened and died. His sister sickened and died, and was buried in such a cheap, rickety funeral that two horrified cabmen refused to follow the coffin for fear of losing their reputations as decent citizens. Working twelve hours a day with pick and shovel, and putting half the night into saving Ireland, Sean sickened more than once and went into a hospital as a charity patient, where he got the first good food he had ever tasted.

But the passion of a fiery Irishman drove him on — passion for poetry, passion for songs, passion for causes, passion for ideas. He was full of scorn, bitterness and hatred. But he was also full of songs; he loved flowers — 'the golden-headed musk, the purple-belled fuchsia'; and he was wondrously observant about everything that came his way. Restless, intolerant, quarrelsome, he beat his way through a poverty-ridden life, acknowledging only the nobility of his aging mother, who lived on a pitiful pension, and of the Reverend E.M. Griffin, rector of St Barnabas, who knew in his bones what life was about. It is only a lucky accident that a man like O'Casey has reported in plays and now in his autobiography the things he knows to be true. For in his case writing is only incidental to the great job of keeping wholly alive.

O'Casey at Bat*

FOURTH VOLUME IN A VIVID AUTOBIOGRAPHY BY A GIFTED DUBLIN DRAMATIST

Although nobody seems to realize it, Sean O'Casey has been writing his autobiography during the past ten years — writing it, moreover, with genius. The first volume, *I Knock at the Door*, is the most beautifully perceptive book I have read about the touching, wondrous experience of coming into an adult world and blundering around in search of a place in society. None of the other three volumes, including *Inishfallen, Fare Thee Well*,

---

* *The New York Times* (27 Feb. 1949).

which has just come from the Macmillan's press, has the sublimity of the childhood volume, though in all of them, the prose is superb, the spirit is fiery and the portraits of Dublin and her people are vivid.

Yet the lack of interest in the O'Casey series is remarkable. *I Knock at the Door* sold less than two thousand copies in this country and is out of print; *Pictures in the Hallway*, the same. *Drums under the Windows* did a little better: it sold nearly three thousand copies. In the meanwhile, Mr O'Casey, generally recognized as the foremost Irish dramatist of his time, has written a number of plays that have gone unproduced in this country and, with one minor exception, in England and Ireland also — *Purple Dust*, *The Star Turns Red*, *Red Roses for Me*, *Oak Leaves and Lavender* and *Cock-a-Doodle Dandy*.

Since plays are a good deal more expensive and difficult to produce than books and since Mr O'Casey is not exactly a discreet or comfortable author, it is not so remarkable that all his plays have not been produced. He knows they are difficult to put on. But the record is curiously bleak for a man of his gifts and reputation. Not a single new play by Mr O'Casey has been put on in New York since *Within the Gates* in 1934, which is fifteen years ago. He is author of at least two dramas commonly regarded as masterpieces, *Juno and the Paycock* and *The Plough and the Stars*, and of another drama less commonly regarded as a masterpiece, *Within the Gates*. A number of writers with very much less talent obviously interest the public a great deal more.

Like the three preceding volumes, *Inishfallen, Fare Thee Well* is written in the third person, recording the thoughts, opinions and experiences of one Sean Casside, a Dublin firebrand who became a writer. The new volume takes him through the years when the Abbey Theatre put on *Juno and the Paycock* and *The Plough and the Stars* to the time when he left Ireland forever in self-imposed exile. It includes a masterly sketch of his mother's death in a moldy tenement and of her poverty-stricken funeral, and a memorable character portrait of Lady Gregory — 'a robin with the eye of a hawk.'

These are the two people Mr O'Casey most loved and admired, and what he writes about them is the most eloquent part of the book. In the earlier volumes he has drawn the portrait of his mother with infinite tenderness, recognizing her indomitable spirit throughout a lifetime of adversity in the Dublin slums that swallowed up most of her children. Now Mr O'Casey puts her to rest with sadness, humility and devotion.

He came to know Lady Gregory when the Abbey Theatre was putting on his plays. Since she was the mother of the theatre and all its people were her children, Mr O'Casey's affection for her is filial also. 'Blessed Bridget O'Coole' he calls her. Once he did surprise her when she was reading *Peg o' My Heart*, which, to the puritanical young playwright, seemed like an act of original sin. But she is one of his few heroines — a kindly, immensely cultivated woman who overflowed with affection and goodwill; and Mr O'Casey returns these gifts in the pages he has posted to her memory.

Toward Yeats he has grudging respect. Yeats stood up for Mr O'Casey bravely when the hoodlums of Dublin were heaving fruit and eggs at one of his plays. But the ease, assurance and social grace of professional men of letters irritate Mr O'Casey, who lived in the slums and hates the gentry; and if it were not for Yeats' courage under fire, it is likely that Mr O'Casey would cosign him to oblivion with only a little less scorn than he has for A.E.

This is not a soothing book. Mr O'Casey is a bitter man. He has not forgiven the world for the misery and starvation of the life in the slums which destroyed most of his brothers and sisters and constantly harried his mother. It affected him too. Lack of food undermined his health and almost destroyed his eyesight. In his sixties Mr O'Casey is blind in one eye and sees dimly through the other.

He is against gentility of all kinds. In a swift sketch of [Eamonn] De Valera, Mr O'Casey sets forth in a negative comment his specifications for the ideal human being: 'He [the author] could not see De Valera abandoning himself to sweat and laughter in the dancing of a jig, nor could he see him swanking about in sober green kilt and gaudy saffron shawl; or slanting an approving eye on any pretty girl that passed him; or standing, elbow on counter in a Dublin pub, about to lower a drink, with a Where it goes, lads.'

In a state of rebellion against bourgeois respectability, the dogma of the Catholic Church and political demagoguery, Mr O'Casey imagines that he is a Communist. There could hardly be a more unlikely candidate than this highly individualistic rebel. For the bourgeois respectability, the dogma and the political demagoguery have settled in the USSR, too, and life there has little of the convivial companionship he describes in his comment on De Valera. Harshest of the realistic dramatists, Mr O'Casey is a romantic at heart. There is no physical refuge anywhere for people like him.

But there is a spiritual refuge — art; and that is the one Mr O'Casey has taken. He is writing the most glorious English prose of his time. It has the gusto of the Elizabethans and the music of the Irish. It is savage and caustic, but it is also rich in song and loveliness. It is irascible and joyous. It not only states the facts tersely, but it captures the mood with lyricism and relish. It is angry because it is founded in love and tenderness, which are the basic qualities of Mr O'Casey's character. Personally removed from all the battles he has fought and all the enemies he has made, Mr O'Casey is transmuting a hard life into a prose work of art that is next door to poetry. It is astonishing that so few people are interested in what he is doing.

O'Casey in England*
ROSE AND CROWN ALSO INCLUDES VISIT HERE

After pegging away at his autobiography for the last thirteen years, Sean O'Casey has pushed it along to the time of *Within the Gates*, which was acted in New York in 1934. *Rose and Crown*, he calls this, the fifth volume, published in London by Macmillan during the summer and scheduled to be published here by Macmillan next month. As things have been working out for Mr O'Casey in the meager years since he emigrated to England, this whirling chronicle of a fiery particle may be his most enduring work.

For the author of *Juno and the Paycock* and *The Plough and the Stars*, which stood Dublin on its ear in the twenties, has been our most conspicuously unemployed dramatist for a couple of decades. The most magnificent prose writer in the modern theatre has been left, like a hibernating bear, to suck his own

* *The New York Times* (14 Sept. 1952).

claws in his cave in Devon. Most of his later plays have been written for a sort of mystical, virtuoso theatre that does not exist commercially in New York or London, and their neglect can be explained in terms not only of dollars and pounds, but of actors and directors. But the fact remains that a stage writer whose personal genius is generally recognized has almost no association with the stage, and about as much income from the stage as an apprentice playwright might get if he were lucky. The theatre is the cruellest of the arts and professions.

Rose and Crown is the fifth volume in an autobiography of a spirit. Like its predecessors, this one is told in the third person and without dates. Since it refers to a number of public events, like the Abbey Theatre's rejection of *The Silver Tassie* and Mr O'Casey's memorable visit to America to help stage *Within the Gates*, his cavalier attitude toward chronology is sometimes confusing to a reader who wants to know what happened. *Rose and Crown* looks a little as though it were written in sections: after apparently finishing with the material of one section Mr O'Casey dips back into it later on.

You think that he has finished with poor old James Fagan, who wanted to be his friend and counsellor, but, no, Mr O'Casey still has a gibe or two left in his notebook. Yeats' rather patronizing rejection of *The Silver Tassie* has left a permanent scar on Mr O'Casey's soul, partly because Mr O'Casey is thoroughly aware of Yeats' qualities of greatness as a poet and servant of the arts. *The Silver Tassie* affair keeps popping up all through the book.

(Incidentally, so far as the style and point of view of *The Silver Tassie* are concerned, Mr O'Casey comes out of that brawl more honorably than Yeats. Yeats and the Abbey Theatre were not prepared for such a radical shift from the realistic style of the earlier plays. The contemporary theatre, having learned how to act poetic and subjective plays, knows how to act *The Silver Tassie*, and audiences are not bewildered by its violent shifts in mood.)

But dates and events are not the important things in Mr O'Casey's autobiography. Written like pure literature in a musical style with songs and golden imagery, it expresses the pugnacious, uncompromising spirit of a natural rebel who 'wants to see life, to hear life, to feel life and to use life; to engender in oneself the insistent and unbreakable patience to remove any obstacle life chanced to place in its own way.' That is his basic program.

At least from the worldly point of view it is not a success story but a story of failure. Mr O'Casey and his wife have almost always had a hard time making both ends meet, and he has been generally rejected as a dramatist and political counsellor. *Rose and Crown* is the ebullient record of the impressions the world has made on a sentient spirit that looks through, around and beyond cities and people and keeps soaring above the workaday world.

Nothing is static or literal. Everything is constantly in motion — the cities struggling to contain their people, the people going through a series of social masquerades in company with other people, rich and poor, pious and profane, gentle and rude, Conservatives and Laborites ducking and weaving, with communism, idealized into a sort of holy mass mysticism, providing the ground swell. Although Mr O'Casey likes to visit great houses and has kind words for the gentry who have been friendly, he rigidly divides society into the haves and have-nots. It will be interesting to read what he has to say in later volumes about the social structure of post-war England.

Since the autobiography is more art than history, the proportions and the symmetries have real value. And the brittle tone of some parts of *Rose and Crown* suggests that Ireland provides a better background for Mr O'Casey's troubles and encounters than England does. In Ireland his enemies were combative; the whole place was in a constant uproar and the spiritual drama of Mr O'Casey's life was teeming and resonant.

But England is too tolerant to make a lively protagonist. Mr O'Casey has to supply all the energy from his own spirit. In England his enemies politely disappear before he can fairly get his hands on them. Stanley Baldwin slopes off, smoking his pipe, after Mr O'Casey has confounded him with Irish riddles at an opulent Conservative party reception; Ramsay MacDonald cautiously evades a private meeting with this firebrand, and even Bernard Shaw emerges as a man of prudence. Although the central character in *Rose and Crown* is as vivid as ever, the minor characters are more laconical and fidgety. They do not seem to know what to make of the fiery particle that has come over from Ireland and burned holes in the discreet fabric of their lives.

Some of them probably do not realize that any holes have been burned. But they are wrong. For at the age of sixty-eight, Mr O'Casey is full of life, dreams, bitterness and eloquence. The burning things he has not been able to say on the stage he is now saying in this long autobiography that began in 1939 and is not finished yet. It is an extraordinary piece of dramatic literature written in the most incandescent prose of our time.

Himself, and Things that Happened*
SUNSET AND EVENING STAR

With *Sunset and Evening Star*, Sean O'Casey completes his autobiography. The six-volume series began fifteen years ago with his valiant and lovely impressions of childhood, *I Knock at the Door*. In that book 'Johnny Casside,' as the chief character was then named, innocently entered the slum world of Dublin. In *Sunset and Evening Star* (another glorious title) the chief character is named 'Sean'. He reports some of the things he did and many of the things he thought between his return to England from America and the years following World War II. Since the autobiography is no chronicle of vital statistics, Mr O'Casey is chary of dates. But the period covered in the new volume is from 1934 or 1935 to, apparently, 1949 or 1950.

Whatever else the autobiography may be, it is a masterpiece of writing. The writing has music, eloquence, passion, bitterness and force. It can recreate sense perceptions with concrete exactitude. As an example of Mr O'Casey's descriptive writing with its vivid use of details, note this sentence about an English nursing home where Mrs O'Casey was a patient: 'The rooms were heavy with old air, and wore a weak look, as if they, too, were sick; and all he saw seemed to whisper cynically of uncleanliness and of clumsy, uncomely methods of management and care.'

Or consider this description of the flower-strewn fields of Devon, where the O'Caseys live: 'Newly ploughed fields of red earth, spreading out in a view as wide as the eye can cover, aglow

* *The New York Times* (11 Nov. 1954).

with their differing hues, from reddish-purple, reddish-brown to
what seems to be a vivid crimson, separated here and there by
squares and diagonals of green as rich and velvety as the red, a
sight to be wondered at and loved. Oh, the Devon people have a
beautiful carpet under their feet.'

Mr O'Casey has long been fascinated by the mystical prose style
of James Joyce, whom he regards as a master of writing. There are
more than the usual number of Joycean passages in *Sunset and
Evening Star*, and it must be conceded that Mr O'Casey manages
them well. When he takes wing into one of these records of
sensory impressions, interwoven with subjective comment, he
keeps one foot on the ground. Whether they are Joyce or Carlyle
might be closely argued. But they do give Mr O'Casey an
opportunity to convey overtones of scorn for the rich, horror of
the inhumanity of bombing, contempt for his enemies. Their
flow of imagery is his comment — generally ironic — on the facts
or the people with whom he is dealing.

It seems to me that the impressionistic passages are second-best
O'Casey. The best O'Casey, which is also the best in modern
English prose, is the direct statement of what happened, like the
hilarious chronicle of a cold night at Cambridge University where
Mr O'Casey got lost in an unlighted corridor; or, the description
of Shaw and Mrs Shaw at the luncheon table, with a record of
what they said. Mr O'Casey is not a self-conscious stylist. The
strength and beauty of his writing are implicit in the purpose of
his autobiography: 'The idea of setting down some of the things
that happened to himself; the thoughts that had darkened or
lightened the roads along which he had traveled; the things that
had woven his life into strange patterns, with the words of a song
weaving a way though a ragged coat, or a shroud, maybe, that
has missed him and covered another.'

Through all his works Mr O'Casey has one theme. He is for joy
and freedom. He hates anything or anyone who does not
contribute to the joy of being alive or who impinges on personal
freedom. He hates gentility because he suspects that it is joyless.
He hates wealth and power because he believes that they are
bought at the expense of ordinary people. Never having been in
the Soviet Union, he wistfully imagines that joy and freedom for
all the people will grow like a beautiful flower out of the wide
land where the slave camps flourish. Never was there a man less
suited by temperament to the harsh disciplines of Soviet society.

r O'Casey is not one to abandon old ideals lightly. One of the most pungent chapters in *Sunset and Evening Star* portrays his imperious dismissal of a former Soviet worker who has the effrontery to tell him that the Ogpu took her husband away. 'Not proven,' is Mr O'Casey's lofty verdict. 'Lady,' said Sean [to quote what he has written], 'I have been a comrade of the Soviet Union for twenty-three years, and all she stands for in the way of socialism, and I don't intend to break that bond for a few hasty remarks by one who obviously hates the very bones of the Soviet people. And the more you shout, lady, the less I hear.'

Pegging away at his writing in Totnes, Mr O'Casey is not inclined to have an old faith shaken by an overwrought woman back from Russia whose husband had been spirited away by the police. He dislikes her so much he probably suspects that her husband conspired with the police to get away from home. He dismisses her from his house with a royal gesture.

Despite the grandeur of the writing, *Sunset and Evening Star* is a quarrelsome book. When Mr O'Casey is not relating what happened to himself and his family, he carries on a running feud with the Roman Catholic Church, to which he keeps returning; G.K. Chesterton, whom he regards as a fake; Denis Johnston, who was so ignorant that he did not recognize a Giorgione picture hanging in the O'Casey hallway (a good example of the O'Casey snobbery in reverse); George Orwell, who reviewed *Drums under the Windows* contemptuously, and other people and institutions that Mr O'Casey keeps on his griddle. These tirades, some of them as furious as tracts, become tiresome before the book is finished. But they are part of the O'Casey temperament and have to be borne, though not necessarily in silence.

One reason they grow tiresome is that Mr O'Casey is also a warm-hearted, gentle man, affectionate toward his family and his friends, and he is spiritually unconquerable. There is plenty of the lovable O'Casey in these pages. Note, especially, his compassionate understanding of the needs of children; his devotion to the memory of his mother, who was the immortal character in the early books; his sorrowful portrait of a Totnes mother who had just lost her son in battle; his loyalty to Lady Gregory; his respect for Yeats; his kindly interest in the American soldiers quartered in Totnes during the war; his humility toward his wife.

In all his moods there is one dominant fact about Mr O'Casey.

He is thoroughly alive. In his seventies, he is still a fiery particle. He is not giving quarter on any side. Laying down his worn pen in the sixth volume of his story, he writes this word of farewell: 'Here, with whitened hair, desires failing, strength ebbing out of him, with the sun gone down, and with only the serenity and calm warning of the evening star left to him, he drank to Life, to all it had been, to what it was, to what it would be. Hurrah!'

He's a man.

Part IV
The Essays

Feudist with a Song in his Heart*

Rummaging around among his old papers Sean O'Casey has assembled the materials for a book. In an amiable introduction, written last spring when the birds were singing he calls the book *The Green Crow* in recognition of his own capacity for cawing.

'Some Latin writer said, "If a crow could feed in quiet, it would have more meat,"' Mr O'Casey observes. But he has never been able to keep quiet, he remarks and so the Green Crow 'has had less meat than it might have had if only it had kept its big beak shut.'

Although the voice is that of a crow, the nest is that of a magpie. It contains bits and pieces collected at random. About half of the bits are roars of rage at critics — Irish critics who drive Mr O'Casey out of his wits, and British critics, who merely infuriate him. Fortunately, the American critics do not provoke him into such fits of cawing. They are further removed from Devon, where the Green Crow makes his nest and feeds his fledglings.

If memory serves, most of the fulminations against critics first appeared in 1936[1] in *The Flying Wasp*, a venomous volume. Although they are written in a state of Irish fury, the plays to which they refer are so minor that the fury seems querulous now. Mr O'Casey's torrid tract against Noel Coward, twenty-nine pages long, also sounds peevish now.

Lest you suspect that the Green Crow speaks more temperately today, take warning, lads. There is a sizzling attack on the Dublin critics who took a hostile view of Mr O'Casey's *The Bishop's Bonfire* only last spring. The Green Crow begins his attack with characteristic furor: 'Fire, fire, fire! Where? Who done it? Who do you think done it? O'Casey done it.' Through another twenty-nine pages he gives the Dublin scribblers a scorching foretaste of hell. *The Bishop's Bonfire* was never so hot as Mr O'Casey's

The New York Times (18 Mar. 1956).

retort. 'And where's and how's O'Casey after the flarum harum
scarum of "The Bishop's Bonfire"?' he inquires in his concluding
paragraph. 'At home, thank ye, and safe. A bit broody, trying to
think out if he be the right man with the wrong ideas, or the
wrong man with the right ideas...'

Since scandal is always more fascinating than sense, it would be
easy to attach too much importance to Mr O'Casey's feuds and so
underestimate the fine things that turn up in this volume. They
include: fresh and perceptive appreciations of Shaw and Shakespeare; a grand, humorous salute to St Patrick's Day; some penetrating criticism of naturalism in the theatre and the obsolete
proscenium arch; a wholesome, heart-rending recognition of the
artistic sense that is born into every child; and four short stories,
in two of which Mr O'Casey pokes into the privacy of the human
soul with compassion and understanding. 'The Star-Jazzer' and 'A
Fall in a Gentle Wind' are simple in design and noble in feeling,
and among the finest things he has written.

Who is this Green Crow who sets up a fearful clatter and can
also sing as sweetly as the nightingale? He is a skinny, warm-
hearted, near-sighted, pipe-smoking Irishman of 76 years who
lives on next to nothing with an affectionate family in an upstairs
flat in Torquay by the sea. He is a profoundly religious man who
would be satisfied to call himself a rationalist if he did not find
himself loving so many of the wonders of life. Art is something he
reveres with holy adoration — not only writing and theatre, but
music and painting. He is also a dedicated student of history,
religion, literature and everything that concerns humanity. He
was a Communist 'long, long before I ever heard the name of
Lenin,' he says. 'I am a Shelleyan Communist and a Dickensian
one and a Byronic one and a Miltonian one and a Whitmanian one
and one like all those who thought big and beautifully and who
cared for others, as I am a Marxian one, too.'

Although he lives in England his heart is in Ireland. He can
telephone to Dublin for two shillings sixpence from his flat. Since
he can write like an angry bull, some people are afraid of him.
But there was never a more modest, gentler-mannered man with
a kindlier feeling for people. As a writer he will make no compromises for money. He has had to make some hard financial
decisions 'to remain true to himself and right with God,' but he
has make them without whining. As an old man he is merrier
than he was as a chisler, for he is full of hope. Not so much for

himself, however, as for other people. Although the Green Crow screams, there's not a mean bone in his body.

NOTES

1. 1937.

Critic at Large*

A NEW BOOK OF ESSAYS BY SEAN O'CASEY SHOWS GREEN CROW PUNGENT AS EVER

Here comes the Green Crow wearing a colored cap. *Under a Colored Cap* is the bright title of Sean O'Casey's new book of essays that Macmillan has published in London. (It will be published here by St Martin's Press June 14.)

Seven years ago Mr O'Casey reported that some Latin writer had said that if a crow could feed in quiet he would have more meat. Mr O'Casey found this bit of natural lore irresistible. Throughout the years he believes he might have had more meat if he had been able to keep his big beak shut; and he, accordingly, dubbed himself 'The Green Crow' in a book of fulminations. Note that he was 'The Flying Wasp' in his earliest book of fulminations in 1937.[1]

Now he is 84 years old, frail, nearly stone blind, like Old Gobbo, and generally confined to a third-floor flat in Torquay, England. 'I have been shoved down into the chair by the push-push of many years,' he declares in the pungent style that is characteristic. To ward off drafts he now wears skull caps. In recent years these particular colored beanies have become as much a part of his costume as the familiar turtleneck sweater. Although Mr O'Casey is not a snappy dresser, he never looks dull.

When the book was in proof last winter, he was afraid that it would indicate that he had lost his capacity for belligerence. He

The New York Times (17 May, 1963).

had meekly removed some sentences and phrases that his publisher's solicitor regarded as libelous. But Mr O'Casey need not have worried. His subjects today may be more remote and tenuous than they were in the days when he was getting around freely. Now he has to set up some straw men to belabor. But he is still a bellicose member of the disloyal opposition.

There is one noble exception to his series of ambushes. The essay entitled 'Under a Greenwood Tree he Died' is a moving requiem to his son, Niall, who died of leukemia several years ago.[2] Naill had come home for Christmas, apparently in the best of health. Within a fortnight he was gone. 'Death cut down the vigorous young sapling,' says his father, 'and left the gnarled old tree standing, left the gnarled, old, withering tree standing.' Since writing can be a form of therapy, Mr O'Casey wrote the whole sad story in all its homely detail while the grief was still unbearable. None of the O'Casey family has recovered from this inexplicable calamity.

Most of the book consists of jeremiads against people and institutions that, in Mr O'Casey's opinion, misrepresent life as dismal and hopeless. In his middle eighties he is all for a song and a dance in the robust style of the Elizabethans. The cynicism of today he describes as 'sly, mean and commonplace.' Since Shakespeare did not use despair to inflate his ego, Mr O'Casey regards many contemporary writers as lacking in compassion and as poseurs in a modish style. When he reviews the achievements that have occurred in his lifetime, the Green Crow cannot help feeling hopeful.

There is a note of particular relish in the caws he directs at organized religion. Since in his opinion churches, and specifically the Roman Catholic Church, deny life its simple pleasures, he continues his familiar vilification of prelates and dogma. He is so acid about them that he can make the title 'His Grace the Archbishop' sound like an epithet.

One cannot read Mr O'Casey through the years without nothing that he loves the literary rites of religion. His works are saturated with rich phrases like 'Mass, matins and Evensong' which he fondles on his pen. Like James Joyce, a renegade Catholic, Mr O'Casey, who was born a Protestant, is steeped in the lore of churches. Although he 'cannot believe' that there is a God, God is frequently his measure of the goodness of man.

When Mr O'Casey takes pen in hand, the trolls take charge of him. Many contrary notions whirl around under his colored cap on a hill in Torquay. In 84 years he has absorbed a lot of pain and disappointment. But he refuses to be downhearted. The concluding three lines of some verse in one of his essays are:

> Caw Caw Caw Caw
> A herald angel sings,
> An' evenin's full of th' green crow's wings.

NOTES

1. *The Flying Wasp* (1937), a collection of essays, many of which were reprinted in *The Green Crow.*
2. 1956.

Part V
In Passing

Paradox of O'Casey*

HE IS ONE OF THE GREAT MODERN WRITERS BUT HIS PLAYS ARE SELDOM PERFORMED

For the last several weeks an organization dubbed Theatre Today has been acting Sean O'Casey's *The Plough and the Stars* in an airtight dungeon off Twenty-sixth Street. Since the truth has to be printed in this column now and then to hold the franchise, it is necessary to point out that Theatre Today is unable to do a very good job. Perhaps that impression is due partly to the fact that many of us still hear in O'Casey's sinewy lines the echoes of some great theatre voices — those of Barry Fitzgerald, F.J. McCormick, Michael Dolan, Maureen Delany, May Craig, Eileen Crowe, Ria Mooney, to mention some of the actors in the old Abbey Theatre company.

Naturally their accents were greener than one has a right to expect of a mixed company like the people in Theatre Today cast. We can do without the true accents if we have to. But the vital contribution of the Abbey Theatre company was the turbulent passion of the characterization and of the performance as a whole. For *The Plough and the Stars* is not merely a ramshackle comedy of the Dublin tenements, but a scream of rage over what O'Casey regards as the shiftlessness, vanity, cruelty, mindlessness, pathos and tragic futility of the Easter uprising in 1916.

Only experts on the intricacies of Irish politics know exactly where O'Casey stood on that issue. Since all his life he has been in a state of rebellion against any kind of authority, presumably he is not opposed to revolution. Look at that thin, pointed jaw which he thrusts ahead of him year after year to give the natural warmth of his heart a weapon. But his portrait of both the motives and the tactics of the Easter uprising is scornful and devastating.

On the higher levels of command there may have been a plan

---

*The New York Times (2 Apr. 1950).

and a practical motive. But O'Casey, an old tenement dweller, wrote *The Plough and the Stars* in terms of his neighbors whose human tenacity he admired. In the play they are the instruments and the victims of the uprising: and on that level *The Plough and the Stars* is horrifying. The Theatre Today performance does fairly well with the pungent comedy scenes, but it is not able to communicate much of O'Casey's disgust. At bottom, *The Plough and the Stars* is a terrifying indictment of a human disaster.

Although O'Casey has not had a professional production on Broadway since *Within the Gates* in 1934, he is generally regarded as one of the great modern writers. As the off-Broadway groups have come to realize, his name is a very attractive one to have on the billboards. Whatever the quality of the current performance of *The Plough and the Stars* may be, Theatre Today has no trouble in selling out every weekend performance. O'Casey was close to being forgotten a decade ago. But he is a man of colossal fortitude. He has kept pegging away all these years; and now everyone who loves writing recognizes him as a genius. Nothing could be more ironic than the contract between his reputation and his success. He is a great writer but his plays are seldom produced.

This is not because of the traditional scorn of publicans for genius. Several producers of taste would very much like to put on one of O'Casey's unproduced dramas. Kermit Bloomgarden, for example, would like to produce *Purple Dust*, which has been available between covers for more than a decade. But it is a difficult play to organize for stage production. For O'Casey has abandoned the realistic forms of *Shadow of a Gunman, Juno and the Paycock* and *The Plough and the Stars*; and, reverting to the style of his first published writing, 'Sound the Loud Trumpet,' he is writing in the form of fantasy. That is what he likes most. Whatever their literary or intellectual values may be, these plays are not easy to perform. They set the stage some very tough practical and artistic problems. O'Casey knows that they do, although he is not the man to make any compromise between what he wants to do and what he knows would be the smart thing to do.

Theoretically, everything good can be staged. If a play is good, there is a way of acting it. Take, for instance, O'Casey's *Cock-a-Doodle Dandy*, which was published by Macmillan last year. It is another variation on O'Casey's primary thesis that people should not be afraid of enjoying life and that institutionalized morality is a denial of life. This is a philosophical idea, as opposed to narrative drama or problem play. O'Casey has composed it as a fantastic comedy with some of the form of a ballet and some of the properties of a magic show. Although it has a few gusty characters it is worked out supernaturally like an adult fairy story.

It can be produced. In fact, Margo Jones has produced it in her enterprising little arena theatre in Dallas, and the reports have been good.[1] She is doubtless the one person who knows most about the problems O'Casey has set the theatre with his whimsical satire on puritanism. In comparison with *The Plough and the Stars*, which raises no unusual stage problems, *Cock-a-Doodle Dandy* is generalized in theme instead of being specific, and it lacks a concrete locale. The texture of the play is soft. Although the writing is sardonically humorous, it lacks the bite, sting, fire and wild temperament of the talk in the tenement houses. It also lacks the earthiness of *Within the Gates*, when O'Casey broke away from the realistic theatre definitely and wrote in the classic form of a masque.

Although O'Casey's reputation is based on his early realistic plays and the on the masterly autobiography that he is still writing, there is no reason why he should try to repeat himself. He is perfectly willing to accept the penalties for working in mediums that are more elusive and difficult and that interest smaller audiences. In *Cock-a-Doodle Dandy* he is not writing out of personal experience. He is on his own, and this is a formidable challenge to even a great writer like O'Casey. It leaves him wholly dependent on personal resources of imagination and spiritual vitality. He has to create not only the theme but the form, the characters and the symbols. Working in this capricious vein, he has to renounce the sturdy support of the visible world.

Cock-a-Doodle Dandy can be played on a Broadway stage with tang, humor and gusto. But it needs uncommonly resourceful direction and acting. It needs genius. In fact, it would help a lot if Barry Fitzgerald played all the parts.

NOTES

1. At 'Theatre 50' in Dallas, Texas, 30 January 1950.

Arts and Dollars*

THOUSANDS FOR RUBBISH BUT NOT FOR O'CASEY

In an adjoining column last Sunday, William Saroyan (Wild Bill to his friends) pointed out that there has not been a professional production of an O'Casey play in this town since 1934, although, to quote him precisely, 'No O'Casey play can be bad in itself.'¹ Mr Saroyan's comment was not an isolated one. The early page proofs of last Sunday's section, which had to be revised, contained a letter to the Drama Editor on the same topic. There was also a brief reference to O'Casey on a general literary subject in this column.

During the previous week the daily news columns had reported that Sam Wanamaker, currently raising the cultural level of drama in London, had bought the rights to Mr O'Casey's *Purple Dust* just in time to prevent the City Center from mounting that comedy here this season. At different times within the past year two college students who are independently writing theses on Mr O'Casey have dropped into this office to talk things over.

To judge by these items and episodes, as well as many items in other periodicals, Mr O'Casey is the most consistently discussed of today's unproduced dramatists. Everyone assumes that he is a dramatist of the first order, if not also a genius, although many of the people who admire him have never seen any of his plays on the professional stage.

If New York producers as a lot put on plays with their own money, one of them before now would have put on *Purple Dust*, which has been available in book form for eight years, or *Cock-a-Doodle Dandy*, which has been available for four. Granted that they are not easy to stage, someone before now would have discovered how to cast and direct them and would have risked a production. For both these plays are obviously the work of a gifted writer who has original ideas, poetic imagination, eloquence and fire. If artistic quality were the only element involved, someone would have taken the plunge before now.

But producers who have tried to raise money for an O'Casey production report that backers do not have much enthusiasm for

The New York Times (11 Jan. 1952).

these dramas. Since the money is theirs they are certainly within their rights when they withhold it from scripts they do not like or regard as risky. And any of the unproduced O'Casey scripts is risky from several points of view, including a reasonable doubt that our theatre is virtuoso enough to perform epic dramas. Ideally, they need a repertory company as versatile as the Barrault troupe that played here earlier in the season.

In the meantime, it is a matter of record that producers have been able to put the bite on backers for such assorted pieces of hokum as *Buttrio Square* and *Whistler's Grandmother*, and an enterprising promoter in Greenwich Village has managed to raise $100,000 to establish a progressive theatre that closed for re-grouping after one performance of *Frankie and Johnny*. Since this column is in the business of criticizing the dramas that finally get on the stage, it is not in an ethical position to tell producers and backers what to put on. But it is entitled to have a low opinion of an industry that cheerfully loses vast sums of money on rubbish and looks down its nose at a genuine artist.

Not that Mr O'Casey makes things any easier. He is a belligerent Irishman who carries about two chips on every shoulder. Hell is likely to break loose whenever one of his plays appears on the stage. There was a riot in Dublin when *Juno and the Paycock* was first acted;[2] and to this day some Dublin critics write about Mr O'Casey with a virulence that could be no more obscene if he had robbed the poor boxes in church vestries or snatched the shawl from Mother mo Chree.

His last professionally produced drama here, *Within the Gates*, was banned in Boston.[3] All hell broke loose in Houston a couple of seasons ago when The Playhouse put on *Red Roses for Me*.[4] From the literary point of view, *Red Roses for Me* is a beautifully written epic drama. But from the intellectual point of view it is priggish if not pedantic, and it has a solemn attitude toward the class struggle that in England and America, at least, is obsolete today. Parochial in outlook, it invites a parochial response. People who have not had a long training in the O'Casey audacity are likely to get nervous when he shoves his literary lever under the base of the universe.

Probably *Oak Leaves and Lavender*, written in 1946, is too intimately bound up with the war to arouse much interest today, although, like all his epic dramas, it is bursting with life. *Purple Dust* and *Cock-a-Doodle Dandy* are the ones that are likely now to be the most acceptable to our theatre — the one a rough-and-tumble vaudeville full of satire and low comedy; the other in magnificently wrought fable about the ancient feud between bigotry and paganism. *Purple Dust* would be the easier to perform in terms of the kind of theatre we have, although it does belabor one joke unmercifully and some of the speeches are too long and intricate. Although ordinary acting and directing would not suffice, *Purple Dust* remains within the range of our professional theatre.

Cock-a-Doodle Dandy (first produced by Margo Jones in Dallas)[5] makes extraordinary demands on the artistic resources of the theatre. It is an improvisation in the form of a comic allegory, fantasticated in style — a Mother Goose story with an adult point of view. To one who has read it at least three times within the last three years, and with increasing admiration, it is Mr O'Casey's finest achievement since he abandoned the realistic form. It is perfectly designed, sensitively written, independent and fearless, full of laughter and wisdom, signifying the joy of being alive. In his late 60s, after a bitter life and a frustrated career, Mr O'Casey transmuted his old theme of love and revelry into a lyric country dance with some innocent feats of magic tossed in for the fun of it. If our dramatic stage were as versatile as our musical stage, *Cock-a-Doodle Dandy* could be a memorable theatre experience.

Thousands of dollars for *Buttrio Square* and *Frankie and Johnny* but not one cent for Sean O'Casey. Mr Saroyan has a right to be indignant.

NOTES

1. William Saroyan, 'Some Frank Talk with William Saroyan,' *New York Times* (4 Jan. 1953) sect. 2, pp. 1, 3.
2. Atkinson is thinking of the world premiere of *The Plough and the Stars*, Dublin, 8 February 1926, which was accompanied by several nights of rioting.
3. See pp. 67–70, Atkinson's article, 'Boston Secedes from the Universe' (27 Jan. 1935).
4. Opened 25 April 1951, directed by John O'Shaughnessy.
5. Theatre '50, Dallas, Texas, 30 Jan. 1950.

Critic at Large*

O'CASEY'S COMMUNISM IS REALLY A DREAM OF A BETTER LIFE FOR MANKIND

In *Sean O'Casey: The Man and His Work* (Macmillan, 1960), nothing is stated more lucidly than David Krause's analysis of O'Casey's adherence to communism: 'One might substitute for O'Casey's Red Star the Star of Bethlehem or the symbol of almost any religion based upon the brotherhood of man.'

To most of us, communism means the dictatorship of a gang of political despots over the Soviet people as well as the people of the satellite states. The bloody annihilation of the Hungarian rebellion in 1956 represents for most of us the true nature of communism.

But O'Casey, a stubborn man, does not permit current realities to intrude into his dream of a better life for all human beings. His communism, he says with the pride of an old believer, goes back beyond Lenin to Milton, Keats, Shelley, Byron, Dickens, Emerson and Whitman — all of them writers, as he is. 'Communism is not to be found in a booklet, but springs to life from within, like the Kingdom of Heaven,' he believes. If Soviet communism were a conclave of saints and scholars, O'Casey would not be surprised, but the rest of us would be mighty elated.

The last volume of his autobiography, *Sunset and Evening Star*, contains an amusing account of his short way with dissenters. One beautiful Sunday afternoon in Devonshire, where he was pondering the problem of God and T.S. Eliot, he was interrupted by the appearance of three middle-aged women, none of whom seemed personally attractive to him. The bell-wether of the flock he calls 'Creda Stern,' although that is not her name.[1]

Having heard that he professes to be a Communist, she bursts in on him with a piece of grizzly news calculated to shake his faith. She and her husband, both British Socialists, had gone to the Soviet Union to help found the perfect state. They held important positions, she says, 'in the Comintern on the Commissariats of Foreign Trade and Light Industries.' But one day the

---

* *The New York Times* (13 Sept. 1960).

secret police took her husband away without warning or accusa-
tions, and she says she has never heard anything from or about
him. 'Now, what do you think of your Soviet Union?' she sarcas-
tically inquires.

He thinks very well of it. 'The more you shout, lady, the less I
hear,' he retorts. As the ladies retire in disgust down the garden
path between beds of hollyhocks and dahlias, he surmises that her
husband 'took a powder' to get away from such an objectionable
woman.

O'Casey is not a member of the Communist Party because, he
says, he does not regard himself as yet worthy of that rank: 'A
man must be first excellent at what his hand findeth to do before
he could be a Communist at all.'

Admirers of O'Casey, of whom I am one, have to accept his
partisanship for Soviet communism as the foible of a man of
literary genius who longs for the millennium, and also has a
psychological need for total alienation from human institutions.

At the time when the Nazis were casting a terrible shadow
across the world, O'Casey wrote a mechanical, humorless, propaganda play, *The Star Turns Red* [1940], which divided the
world into black and red. Produced by a Left Wing group in
London,[2] it made no impression on anyone except the one man
least likely by temperament and experience to tolerate it. The late
James Agate, critic for *The Sunday Times*, pronounced it a
'masterpiece.'[3] Since O'Casey, a few years earlier, had eviscerated
Agate for writing scornfully of *Within the Gates*,[4] Agate's
endorsement of *The Star Turns Red* was generally regarded as an
act of self-defence.

In his other plays and in his autobiography (excepting the
political jeremiads) O'Casey's communism illustrates his private
interpretation of that word: the joy of living, laughter, love for
mankind, hatred for people who impinge on freedom of thought
and spirit, hope for a happy world, peace and brotherhood.

When some American saints and scholars founded Brook Farm
in 1841, they had similar communistic ideals. Brook Farm failed,
as have several other communistic colonies in America. But the
impossible ideals will always remain, lighted, as David Krause
phrases it, by the Star of Bethlehem rather than the star that is
red.

NOTES

1. 'Creda Stern' was Freda Utley (1898–1978), author, lecturer and correspondent on political issues and social conflict. In Moscow, she was a senior scientific worker at the Institute of World Economy and Politics, Academy of Sciences from 1930 until her Russian husband, Arkady Berdichevsky, was arrested by the secret police. He died in a prison camp.
2. The Unity Theatre, 12 March 1940.
3. James Agate, 'A Masterpiece. Unity: *The Star Turns Red* — A Play by Sean O'Casey', *Sunday Times* (17 Mar. 1940) p. 3.
4. See the essays in O'Casey's *The Flying Wasp* (1937).

Critic at Large*

VISIT WITH SEAN O'CASEY; DESPITE INFIRMITIES, GREEN CROW IS STILL IN GOOD FORM

If it were in Sean O'Casey's nature to feel doleful about anything, he would have ample reason.

He is thin and frail. At the age of 83 he has no vision in one eye and very little in the other. He has a spinal infirmity that compels him to lie on the couch in his study a good part of the time.

But nothing depresses the humorous spirit of this indomitable Irish writer, who lives with his indomitable wife, Eileen, in the third floor flat of a suburban house on a hill.

He looks gay. To ward off winter drafts, he wears an embroidered skull cap, which makes him look a little like a chief rabbi, and a red house robe, which makes him look a little like a giddy bishop. Altogether an odd but lively figure as he gropes his way around the room. Smoking Erinmore tobacco in a worn pipe, peering amiably through metal-framed glasses with his one usable eye, he gives an impression of enjoying life and knowing a lot about it in terms of experience, history, religion, art, and theatre literature.

In a new book of essays, to be entitled *Under a Colored Cap*, he will denounce what he regards as W.H. Auden's dismal view of

* *The New York Times* (31 Dec. 1962).

life. 'Life has never been futile for me,' Mr O'Casey observed. 'Of course, there's been a lot of pain in it, but that's a part of it, and I've also enjoyed the fights I have been in.' The manuscript of the new book has just been examined by his publisher's prudent solicitor. A few cautious suggestions have been made. One that Mr O'Casey regrets acceding to is an impertinent sentence in an essay about Kenneth Tynan, drama critic of *The Observer*.

Within the past few years Mr Tynan has had the effrontery to disparage some O'Casey work and make at least one factual error. No man to take anything lying down, Mr O'Casey wrote: 'Mr Tynan has a very bad habit of running too fast in front of his own nose.' Mr O'Casey is sorry to lose a phrase he is fond of. But he does not want to distress his publishers who have been loyal to him for almost 40 years. 'I guess I'm softening up,' he said with a wry grin.

Because of his grievously impaired vision, he finds it difficult to write. Eileen ('God bless her!') helps him as much as she can. But he has to hold his work within a few inches of the one eye that still gives a little vision. If he is interrupted, it takes him 10 or 15 minutes to find the place where he left off. He is working now on the script of a film that John Whiting, a British playwright, has made from the first three volumes of the O'Casey autobiography — *I Knock at the Door, Pictures in the Hallway,* and *Inishfallen, Fare Thee Well.* The film will be entitled *Young Cassidy.*

But Mr O'Casey is unhappy because the text does not use the original dialogue. Out of professional respect for another writer's work, he does not like to tamper with Mr Whiting's text. But in the laborious scrawl of a man who is nearly blind, Mr O'Casey is slowly introducing some of his own dialogue.

Since he has picked many fights and fought valiantly in others, he has a public reputation for combativeness. Essentially, Mr O'Casey is a modest, warm-hearted man with a cheerful soul. He is always surprised when people take offense at his thunderbolts. A few years ago he felt that the archbishop of the Roman Catholic Church in Dublin had insulted Joyce and himself by refusing to offer a votive mass at a festival in which their works were scheduled to appear.[1] Mr O'Casey angrily banned the professional use of his works in Ireland. For several years they have been performed only by amateurs. Although he is still smarting from an old insult, he does not regard the ban as inflexible and may reconsider it for the Dublin theatre festival next autumn.

Although he is full of years and infirmities he is alert and optimistic, with a relish of anything comic. In the winter, the grass is still green in Torquay, and people still work in their kitchen gardens. Although Mr O'Casey is no longer able to see the green woodpecker who visits an old tree in the garden, he enjoys hearing him tap, and he listens to the tawny owl in the evening. The Green Crow, as he once described himself, is in good form. Although his voice is soft, it is spirited.

NOTES

1. *Drums of Father Ned* was scheduled to appear at the Irish festival, *An Tostal*, in May 1958. However, after a public pronouncement by the Most Rev. Dr McQuaid, archbishop of Dublin, that the play probably wasn't suitable for production, O'Casey withdrew the play and banned professional productions of his work in Ireland until 1964, the year of his death.

Critic at Large*

SEAN O'CASEY, NEARLY BLIND, STILL THUNDERS BUT ALWAYS WITH FONDEST GREETINGS

Don't expect Sean O'Casey to truckle for sympathy or to intrude on the world with his private troubles.

Two recent letters from him have avoided specific statements about his eyesight, which has been failing for years. To clarify the record, the London bureau of *The New York Times* asked him the direct question by telephone. 'Possibly I could read an illuminated sign outdoors,' he replied. 'But not ordinary newsprint or the letter text in a book. All the hundreds of books around me are dumb. I can write a little, largely by sense of touch. But I cannot read back what I have put down. I typewrite a little by touch, by guesswork, because I was not taught how to type blind. Fondest greetings.'

'Fondest greetings' is the operative phrase. For the most lovable

* *The New York Times* (14 Apr. 1964).

trait of this Irish writer — 84 years of age last month — is his intellectual and spiritual vitality. He is in there punching. No, the ban on his plays in Ireland has not been 'slid aside.'¹ Out of respect for the Shakespeare 400th anniversary celebration, he has permitted the Abbey Theatre to present two of his plays in Dublin so that the performances will be set when the Abbey does them in England. He also is taking sardonic delight in reports that at the dress rehearsal of *The Plough and the Stars* the old theatre was 'packed out with priests.'

'What an odd scene it must have been,' he says — 'O'Casey surrounded and applauded by priests, and Irish priests, too.'

But once the Shakespeare festival is over O'Casey will once more draw himself to full height, like Cardinal Richelieu, and excommunicate the Irish theatre. 'The Irish drama and the Irish literary intelligentsia in general are clamorous in declaring that the [O'Casey] plays written after *The Plough and the Stars* are worthless and their nonproduction in Ireland "no loss," as well as many references to them which are downright insults,' O'Casey observes.

He loves Ireland more than anything in this world. He also longs to love the Irish church, for he is a godly man and has always been fascinated by church lore and ritual. One of his most cherished friends is the parish priest in Totnes, Devon, where the O'Caseys once lived. 'We practically went through the war years arm in arm,' he affectionately recalls. But every man kills the thing he loves. Back goes the ban, and the back of the O'Casey hand to the priests of Ireland.

Saros Cowasjee, a scholar who lives in Bombay, has just published an appreciative book entitled *Sean O'Casey, The Man Behind the Plays* (St Martin's Press) [1963]. Among its several virtues is Mr Cowasjee's admiration for *Within the Gates* — 'a very rare thing in our theatre: a morality play that is also a work of art.' Some day an inspired troupe of actors may succeed in capturing the exaltation of this shepherd's calendar, set in a city park like Hyde Park in London.

But flattery gets you nowhere with O'Casey. 'Saros Cowasjee's book is full of inaccuracies and several downright libels,' O'Casey reports. 'He has put down a lot of mere gossip heard from ordinary ignorant people, with a number of quotes from Joseph Holloway's notorious diary.' Cowasjee admires the plays that the Irish intelligentsia regard as worthless. But in O'Casey's view that does not absolve him from having believed picturesque things that Irish people — all of them poets — told him in Dublin.

This sounds perverse and crotchety. It is the public mask of a modest, kindly man of wide spiritual vision who has an unconquerable faith in the human race and has consistently stood for freedom and joy. After many years of work and a long, wearing period of privation he now has to peep at life from among shadows, his wife keeping an eye on him 'so that I don't end my life with a bang.' Aside from singing a few songs and speaking a few works into a tape recorder, he has no plans: 'I have gone away from being "a springer of birches."' But when he considers how his light is spent he does not, like the blind John Milton, dolefully conclude that 'They also serve who only stand and wait.' O'Casey is still discharging thunderbolts, but with fondest greetings, as he says.

NOTES

1. See footnote pp. 153–5, in Atkinson's column of 31 December 1962.

Part VI

Sean, Sean, Fare Thee Well

A Darlin' Man*

To me the sad news of Sean O'Casey's death is startling for a
personal reason. His humorous vitality seemed to be inexhaustible.

In the 1920's when *Juno and the Paycock* and *The Plough and
the Stars* were provoking the wrath of the Dublin Irish and the
admiration of the rest of the English-speaking world, O'Casey's
eyesight was already impaired and his physical health was not
rugged. But his spirit was fiery.

Through all the many years until yesterday it remained the
same. He kept on discharging thunderbolts with the vigor of a
man who could never surrender to expediency.

The early plays were the best known to everyone. He had improvised a form of playwriting that combined comedy and
tragedy in a single explosion of feeling. There was no comfort for
anyone in *Juno*, *The Plough* and *Shadow of a Gunman*. Everyone
expected O'Casey to continue writing plays in the same vein of
savage realism about the emotionally volcanic Dubliners with
whom he had lived.

But his rebelliousness extended beyond politics, religion and
national affairs to dramatic forms. Influenced a little by the
literary improvisations of Joyce, he introduced expressionism into
The Silver Tassie. He adapted the classical masque to *Within the
Gates* — a glorious play that has never been sufficiently appre-
ciated. *Purple Dust* was a wild lampoon. In *Cock-a-Doodle
Dandy* he wrote a low comedy fairy story.

Never satisfied with the conventions of civil life, he was never
satisfied with the conventions of drama. Personally he was an
affectionate human being who respected all kinds of people. He
was more openhanded than the state of his exchequer permitted.
But as a writer he was committed to adventure. The relative lack
of success in his later plays disappointed him. But it also drove

* *The New York Times* (19 Sept. 1964).

161

him further into new ground. He could not be consoled with praise of the plays he had written in his youth.

Some demon forced him to alienate himself from all the easy civil relationships. Born not only a Protestant but also a poor Protestant in an Irish Catholic community, he began with two alienations. He alienated himself from the Abbey Theatre by furiously attacking W.B. Yeats for rejecting *The Silver Tassie*. He alienated himself from Ireland by emigrating to England. He alienated himself from most of the English by espousing Russian communism, but he alienated himself from the Communists by declining to join the party and by professing a romantic communism that disciplined Communists could not accept. The fiery period of Sean O'Casey was the one thing he could never surrender.

All this sounds like the portrait of a very uncomfortable person. But the paradox of O'Casey was that he was a modest man of wide and deep sympathies, who loved his family and remained loyal to his friends. He was especially fond of Americans.

Feeling that America had been conspicously patient with him, he loved America this side of idolatry; and the memories he had of his one visit to America in the 1930's became more golden the more he thought about them. He shared the anguish of Americans when President Kennedy was assassinated last November. Although he was bitter about many things, he had the devotion of a friend to the United States.

If it had not been for his unconquerable spirit the last years in his third-storey flat in Torquay, Devon, might have been dismal. He had very little physical strength; he could no longer read the books that surrounded him or enjoy the pictures in his hallways.

But it was a stimulating experience to visit him. The sincerity of his convictions, the humor of his conversation, the wide range of his knowledge gave an impression of great spiritual vitality. A darlin' man, as Joxer said in *Juno and the Paycock*.

Critic at Large*

IN 84 YEARS OF UNSELFISH LIFE, O'CASEY HAD HIS HEART FAIL HIM ONLY ONCE

Perhaps it can be put this way: I knew that like all men Sean O'Casey must die some day. But it never occurred to me that he would. In the thirty years during which I knew him, he surmounted so many disasters that I was forgetting a basic fact of life.

He did not surmount a heart attack last Friday in a Torquay, England, nursing home, where he had been a patient before. The Irishman who wrote the most glorious English of his time has dropped his pen. But today's column is in honor of the personal side of O'Casey — a god of wrath in his public postures but a kindly man with a modest view of himself in private life.

Both the public and the private personalities were authentic. An enemy of everything that corrodes the spirit, he was a belligerent writer. He could be outrageously quarrelsome in print. But at home he was simple, frank, warm and talkative and very civil in the pursuit of an argument. The public fire became a private glow.

When I first met him in New York, when *Within the Gates* was produced, he was a sharp-faced, thin, animated Irishman with thick glasses to compensate for weak eyes. When I last visited him in December 1962, in his cheerful flat on the third floor of a remodeled house on a hill in Devon, he was still sharp-faced and thin. The lenses in his spectacles were still thick, but they could no longer compensate for eyes that had almost lost their vision.

'Joyous' may not be too radiant a word to describe his inner spirit in his last years. He was an optimist about the future of mankind. Despite the many hardships of his life (he once remarked that he regarded himself as a failure) he always enjoyed the experience of being alive: 'Tired, but joyous, praising God for His brightness and the will towards joy in the breasts of men' — to quote a line he once wrote about himself as a tenement boy in Dublin. Although O'Casey aged, he never changed.

Since he had had little formal education and did not pretend to

* *The New York Times* (22 Sept. 1964).

be a scholar, I was always amazed by the range of his knowledge. He seemed to know and relish just about everything in literature, including the Greek and Latin classics. Like most Irishmen, he was steeped in Irish history. He could wrangle about things that had happened in Ireland a thousand years ago as if they had just appeared in the newspapers. He knew English and American history in depth. He loved classical music and all kinds of paintings.

A man who enjoyed being alive in a sentient world, he was observant and knowledgeable about nature. Acknowledging a National Wildlife Federation stamp of the ivory-billed woodpecker, he replied last month: 'We have none of that variety here; but we have three others — the larger and lesser spotted, and the big green bird, a vivid green with a magnificent crimson-crested head. Once a month or so, one of these appears in our garden, hammering away at the trunks of the trees, a hammering that tells me my bird-friend or bird-brother is with us again.'

When he heard that I had visited the redwoods of California, he recalled that Dr Douglas Hyde, first president of the Gaelic League, had found the redwoods 'terrifying.' He went on to argue that the cypresses in his garden (Cupressus macrocarpa) are 'brothers minor' to the great trees of California. Like many people who lose their sight, he had vivid visual memories. One letter he wrote two years ago was a beautifully composed essay about some swallows he had seen in Dublin when he was a laborer in a construction gang.

How he found time to write so many letters to so many people was always a mystery because none of the letters were tossed off without style. In later years, when his sight was dim, a friend typed them for him and his wife, Eileen O'Casey, helped him with everything.

No portrait of Sean would be complete without an expression of admiration for the main talents as well as the devotion of this energetic, good-humored woman. Last March he itemized her household activities as follows: 'Eileen is snatching a little time to read the letters coming to me and a snatch of words from a book now and then, shopping and cooking, dealing with problems that at times disturb Shivaun [the O'Casey daughter] today and Breon [the son] and his family tomorrow, and keeping an eye out to save me from bumping into things, or tripping over them so that I don't end my life with a bang.'

He didn't end his life with a bang. His heart stopped beating. In 84 years of unselfish living it was the first time his heart had failed him.

Sean, Sean, Fare Thee Well*

Among the advertising cards inside a Second Avenue bus the other day there was a gallant declaration by Sean O'Casey: 'I have found life an enjoyable, enchanting, active and sometimes terrifying experience, and I've enjoyed it completely. A lament in one ear, maybe, but always a song in the other.'

A simple summing-up of more than eighty years of living, it made the inside of a New York City bus seem less sullen than usual as it droned along through the surly traffic. Since O'Casey was not a writer of much popular success I was pleased to find his credo posted prominently inside a metropolitan bus where the remarks of famous people are displayed. It affirmed something I have long believed: that O'Casey's greatest achievement was his shining character, and that great characters are irresistible, everywhere.

A frail, thin, almost totally blind man with sharp features, a fighting jaw and a gay spirit, O'Casey died on 18 September 1964 at the age of 84 in Torquay, England, 3,000 miles due east of the Second Avenue bus line. Nothing he had written for many years had startled the world or choked his exchequer. He regarded himself as a failure because he had not sufficiently provided for his family. But especially in this country he is revered, venerated and loved by thousands of people who never knew him but could not help admiring a man of valor and principle. He inspired them by the little mottoes he expressed at random: 'If we keep our senses open to the scents, sounds and sights all around us, we shall have music wherever we go.' He had music and he made music because he believed in the human race.

Affirmative attitudes toward life can be a pose. Many people keep up their courage by refusing to face life candidly. Being skeptical by nature I once questioned the validity of O'Casey's stubborn faith in the consistent progress of mankind and his conviction that a better day was always dawning. There was a time when I would have regarded the valiant conclusion to the last volume of his autobiography as a pose: 'Here, with whitened hair, desires failing, strength ebbing out of him, with the sun gone down, and with only the serenity and calm warning of the evening star left to him, he drank to Life, to all it had been, to what it was, to what it would be. Hurrah!' He wrote that joyous conclusion to the chronicle of a life-time in 1954.

There were plenty of reasons why he could have cursed his fate and shaken his first at the iniquities of life. He was a Dublin slum child. When he was still a lad his father died and left the family destitute. O'Casey had to go to work before he was educated. In his early youth his eyes began to pain him, and they gave him no respite for the rest of his life. In his last years the suffering was constant. 'Most old eyes fade away calmly,' he wrote to me by proxy, 'but mine, due to that early ailment, are like as if they were burning away; but what would be unbearable to others is by long experience bearable to me.'

He could no longer read, which had been the richest part of his cultural life: 'A bright, clear color has faded out of the colored cap,' he said in the sort of imagery that was common speech to him. 'All the hundreds of books around me are dumb.' And he had other ailments that might have broken a less resolute character. In the late winters and early springs he was in and out of hospitals repeatedly with recurrent bronchial troubles; and he was stiffened by lumbago. In 1956 one of his two sons, Niall, died, leaving the whole family desolate. O'Casey's heart was broken but his pride remained intact: 'Well, we shall have to go alone along the rest of the road,' he wrote the next day.

If O'Casey had wanted to count his grievances he had many. He was poor most of his life. Once the income tax bailiffs in England seized his worldly goods, including his typewriter, because he was delinquent in payments. But he never compromised his principles or cried for help. He could have borrowed any amount he needed from Bernard Shaw, who was especially fond of both O'Casey and Eileen O'Casey, his wife. Many years later O'Casey referred to the situation as follows: 'I am a proud lad and rather do without than get what I needed through favor from anyone.' At a period when his fortunes were terribly low he declined an offer to have one of his plays filmed because he did not trust the taste or the ethics of the producer. Not only proud, but cantankerous, he could cut off his nose to spite his face, and frequently did.

From boyhood he knew the worst. The searing line he wrote in *Juno and the Paycock* in 1925 came out of personal knowledge of the cruelties of life: 'Sacred Heart o' Jesus, take away our hearts o' stone, and give us hearts o' flesh! Take away this murderin' hate an' give us Thine eternal love!' If he had wanted to brood on his succession of troubles he had as much to provoke him as Job. But O'Casey was never embittered. Every morning he went to his desk, to write letters unless he had something professional to write: 'To work is the important thing: creative work if you can, productive work if you can't — that is the pursuit of happiness,' he said. For he enjoyed work as he enjoyed singing, poetry, love and laughter.

Despite his poverty this slight man touched with genius had magnanimous ideas about his friends. In the fifties there were a few years when his royalties, chiefly from America, relieved the tensions of his family life. Nothing better illustrates the kindness that flowed out of him than his offer at this time to help a friend. George Jean Nathan had been struck down by a series of strokes that incapacitated him over a long period of time. Later it turned out that Nathan's financial resources were ample. O'Casey did not know that; he had been worrying about the expenses of a long illness. 'By the way, how does he stand financially?' O'Casey inquired. 'If any effort is needed to help him, and is under-taken I'd very much like to give a hundred dollars or so ... I have been anxious about him.' Though the offer was not needed, it was especially generous because, as O'Casey remarked on another occasion, 'one hundred dollars is a very tidy sum in the economy of the O'Caseys.'

Since he was a highly individualistic and arbitrary rebel with no group discipline it was difficult, even a little amusing, to think of him as a communist. But he insisted that he was, even during the barbarous era of Stalinism when Russian writers who did not toe the party line were persecuted or executed. Nothing could have been more alien to O'Casey's humanitarianism than the ruthlessness of Stalinism. But O'Casey was not the sort of man to be either sensible or prudent; he jumped off cliffs with exuberance and abandon.

Not being able to reconcile his character with the brutalities of

Stalinism I once asked him his definition of a communist: 'Anyone who is honest and gives all he can for the community,' he replied. He went on to say that he had learned his communism not only from Marx but from Keats, Whitman and Emerson. In 1890 he bought 'The Works of Emerson' in one volume for a few shillings in a second-hand store in Dublin. Emerson, he said, opened his eyes to communism — a remark that might have surprised Emerson. O'Casey continued: 'I am a Shellyan communist and a Dickensian one and a Whitmanian one and one like all those who thought big and beautifully and cared for others — as I am a Marxian one, too.'

All this seemed to me so disarming but also so eccentric that I once asked his daughter, Shivaun, how she felt about it. She belongs to a skeptical generation and she has traveled more than her father did. His communism did not seem eccentric to her. 'Sean was a humanitarian, a communist and a pure spirit,' she replied. 'He saw a long way into the future and saw things improving all the time. . . . I miss talking to him now; it seems as if a great piece of life and knowledge has gone.' She added that 'he knew very well what was happening in Russia and China, and saw that his ideals were being arrived at quicker there than in other countries, particularly the capitalistic ones.' For Sean, who could not endow his children with worldly goods, was a hero to his own family; familiarity bred love and devotion.

When *Within the Gates* was put on in New York in 1934 O'Casey came to assist with the production. Although the play failed he fell in love with America and for the rest of his life was one of the staunchest overseas advocates and friends that America has ever had. The widespread admiration for O'Casey in this country reflects the admiration he had for America. 'Yours is a mighty, majestic and magnificent land,' he once wrote to me.

If he replied at generous length and with considerable literary grace to all sorts of letters from all sorts of Americans — most of them unknown to him — it was because he was grateful for the hospitality of America at times when the Irish had rejected him and the British found him an uncomfortable neighbor. I find this observation in a letter of 1956: 'For the past four years or so our income has been enough for most of our needs (thanks mainly to the USA). We as a household are mightily beholden to American generosity and God forbid that we should abuse it.'

His knowledge of America expressed his euthusiasm for the

origins and the practices of democracy. 'By God, you've started well with your first men,' he exclaimed. 'Washington, Jefferson and Madison! Columbia scratched her head with lightning.' To him America was 'a world's wonder,' and 'the gigantic generosity and resolution' of the Americans seemed to him admirable. 'The whole damn lot of us are singing Hail Columbia, and seeking shelter, not beneath the wide wings of God, but under the wider wings of the American eagle,' he said in 1959.

He took a personal interest in American affairs, and had to discuss them with somebody. He sent me an airmail letter of congratulations on the first American space flight in 1962, although I had had nothing to do with it except to look at it on television. He sent me a letter of condolence over a disastrous flood in the Mississippi region, although again I was in no way personally involved. No one was more deeply pained by the assassination of President Kennedy. He needed to share his grief with grieving Americans.

Even the Americans who were not personally acquainted with O'Casey seemed somehow to perceive his fondness for this country. All sorts of Americans were attracted to him: students, housewives, actors, playwrights, film directors, newspaper writers, political leftists and also any number of those muddled egotists who fawn on celebrities and inflate their vanity by regarding their thoughts as rare and their problems as unique and out of vanity seek recognition. O'Casey felt a sense of obligation to all of them. At heart a modest man, he suffered fools gladly if they were American.

And the more he reflected on his one visit to America in 1934 and the more letters he received from Americans the more he idolized this country. His benevolence towards our faults was sometimes embarrassing. But it was gratefully accepted by everyone who knew about it. Many ordinary Americans who had no claim on his time or his thought walked around with letters from O'Casey in their pockets and acquired distinction by showing them to their friends. It seemed to me that the cult of O'Casey derived from nothing more mysterious or recondite than the fundamental decency of a kindly man.

In print he could discharge bolts of lightning like a God of wrath. There was a puzzling — but to me entertaining — disparity between the public and the private O'Casey. 'When I take a pen in my hand I don't known what happens but I become

bither,' he said, writing his own brogue. As a young dramatist he
began by striking out at the volatile temperament of the Irish with
a savagery that provoked riots in the old Abbey Theatre and that
turned many Irish against him as long as he lived. In public he
was so combative that the thin jaw looked like a weapon.

To Noel Coward and James Agate, who were the targets of his
contempt in *The Flying Wasp* in 1937, O'Casey must have
seemed like a monster; they had done him no harm but he vilified
them as if they were enemies. Although his remarks must have
seemed outrageous to them they seemed all in good fun to
O'Casey who prefaced his tirade by describing it as 'a laughing
look-over' with 'many merry and amusing comments.' Since he
had no hard feelings against his victims he was surprised when
they took offense.

Dame Quickly described Falstaff's nose as 'sharp as a pen.' All
the world knows that the man behind the nose was humorous.
Although O'Casey's nose was sharp as either a pen or a rapier it
protruded from the face of a humorous man. O'Casey was hard-
headed and sharp-tongued and a belligerent enemy of cant and
injustice but he was essentially kind-hearted; and his later plays,
like *Cock-a-Doodle Dandy* and *The Bishop's Bonfire*, were
humorous and larkish. In print he never gave the Irish Catholic
Church a moment's peace.

But during World War II one of his cronies was an Irish priest
who used to sit through the bombings with him and rail against
the stupidities of war. In his private life O'Casey was sociable and
entertaining. After he had died I was pleased to receive a letter
from an elderly Irishman who had worked with him on the
Dublin docks when both of them were young. What he
remembered was reassuring: In the Dublin slums the O'Casey's
were 'a most respectable family,' he observed. Also he recalled
that O'Casey amused his fellow dock workers 'with his wit and
wonderful knowledge that met with great respect.' What O'Casey
had written about his youth in *Mirror in My House* I felt was
confirmed by this affectionate letter from a man who had been
there.

Despite the meagerness of his worldly success in the last thirty
years of his life O'Casey never surrendered his faith in the
essential goodness of life. He felt himself surrounded with
wonders and glories. As he went 'swirling' (his word) around the
streets of the St Mary church section of Torquay, where he lived,

the beauties and the complexities of life astounded him. It seemed to him remarkable that life could embrace everything from the huge elephant to the tiny flea, to say nothing of the bacillus and 'the damned virus.' It seemed to him that life was so fantastic that writers and artists did not need to invent anything more remarkable. Although his life had been hard he was always laughing, whistling and singing: 'There are still many red threads of courage, many golden threads of nobility woven into the tingling fibres of our common humanity,' he said at the age of eighty-four in an essay he wrote for the *Atlantic* only a few weeks before his death. The style was a bit labored but the faith was as fresh and exultant as ever.

In some mysterious way (for neither his plays nor his books reached wide audiences) Americans discovered him and admired the vigor and uprightness of his spirit. They recognized in him the faith they seek for themselves. He was a natural believer. The motto posted inside the Second Avenue bus was a statement of fact except in one small detail. It was true that he listened to the lament in one ear, but he sang the song he heard in the other.

NOTE

* *Idea and Image*, Charter Issue (1967).

For Further Reading*

Books about Sean O'Casey
REVIEW of Saros Cowasjee, *Sean O'Casey: The Man Behind the Plays* (1964), 14 Apr. 1964, p. 34.
REVIEW of David Krause, *Sean O'Casey: The Man and His Work* (1960), 7 Aug. 1960, p. 1 (Book Review Section).
REVIEW of *Juno* (musical), 10 Mar. 1959, p. 41.
REVIEW of *I Knock at the Door* (adaptation by Paul Shyre), 19 Mar. 1956, p. 27.
REVIEW of *Pictures in the Hallway* (adaptation by Paul Shyre), 28 Mar. 1956, p. 23; (23 Sept. 1956) sect. 2, p. 1; (28 Dec. 1959) p. 19; (3 Jan. 1960) sect. 2, p. 1.
REVIEW of *Young Cassidy* (film), 6 Apr. 1965, p. 36.

Shorter Reviews of O'Casey Productions
'O'Casey's Dublin Tenements: *Juno and the Paycock Revived Downtown*', at the Greenwich Mews Theatre, 24 Feb. 1950.
'The Play' (on *A Pound on Demand* and *Androcles and the Lion* by the American Repertory Theatre), 20 Dec. 1946.
'A Note on Reviewing' (on *The Flying Wasp*), 6 June 1937.

* *New York Times*

172

Index

This collection of articles spans the careers of Brooks Atkinson and Sean O'Casey. Only a year after Atkinson took over 'The Play' column in the *New York Times*, O'Casey's second published play, *Juno and the Paycock,* arrived in New York for its first American production. In 1968, four years after the dramatist's death and a year before the critic retired, Atkinson wrote the last of his articles on O'Casey.

Students and admirers of O'Casey will find Atkinson's writings on the dramatist invaluable. The critic reviewed nearly all of O'Casey's works which appeared in book form; he was the only critic to review the complete six-volume autobiography; and nobody has reviewed more of the New York stage productions of the playwright's works. Atkinson's writings convey the excitement that greeted the raw power and linguistic beauty of the dramatist's early and most successful plays as they arrived for their New York premières in the 1920s and 1930s. Later, as O'Casey expanded his drama with new and startling literary experiments, the critic was there to record the success or failure of each milestone.

Irish drama enthusiasts will also find Atkinson's writings on O'Casey informative. In their day the Abbey Theatre Players were perhaps the most talented collection of English-language performers in the world. As well as performances in New York they always included an O'Casey play in the repertoire on their frequent tours of the United States. Atkinson's incisive comments on Barry Fitzgerald, F. J. McCormick, Sara Allgood, and others add greatly to our understanding of the power and versatility of these players.

Aspiring drama critics, actors and directors will find this collection of reviews essential to an appreciation of their craft. Atkinson was the undisputed master of dramatic criticism and his writings reflect the best of journalistic skills. Those directly involved in the theatre will find an esteemed critic who was knowledgeable in all aspects of their art.